EST. | 1788

FOUNDERS and FAMOUS FAMILIES
CINCINNATI

Dedicated with love to the memory of
Professor Louis Russell Thomas:
historian, musician, friend.

EST. | 1788

FOUNDERS and FAMOUS FAMILIES

CINCINNATI

by

Wendy Hart Beckman

CLERISY PRESS

*I would like to thank Tina L. Neyer, Wes Gilbert,
Kathleen Nolan, Patia Tabar, and Deb Rieselman
for their content and editing suggestions.*

Founders and Famous Families: Cincinnati

Copyright © 2014 by Wendy Hart Beckman

For further information, contact the publisher at:

Clerisy Press
306 Greenup Street
Covington, KY 41011
clerisypress.com
a division of Keen Communications, Birmingham, Alabama

ISBN 978-1-57860-521-7; eISBN 978-1-57860-522-4

Distributed by Publishers Group West
Printed in the United States of America
First edition, first printing

Front cover photos: (top) iStock/Getty © Davel5957; (bottom) from *The Queen City in 1869* by George E. Stevens, Library of Congress
Back cover photos: © Jeff Kubina/Flickr, https://creativecommons.org/licenses/by-sa/2.0/,https://www.flickr.com/photos/kubina/134592602/in/photolist-6T2oTc-6T2oBp-6T2otn-6T6qfq-LUkV-cTPkz-cTPG7-82XKf-82XEi
Interior illustration credits: pp. 9, 13, 20, 39, 59, 71, 82, 87, 89, 115, 117, 121, 122, 135, 145, 147 © iStock/Getty © Duncan1890
pp. 73, 75, 77 © iStock/Getty © andipantz
pp. 111 , 159 © iStock/Getty © lestyan4

Text and cover design: Travis Bryant

The author is donating 5 percent of her royalties to the Cincinnati Museum Center.

CONTENTS

. . . And this Song of the Vine,
This greeting of mine,
The winds and the birds shall deliver,
To the Queen of the West,
In her garlands dressed,
On the banks of the Beautiful River.

—from "Catawba Wine," by Henry Wadsworth Longfellow, 1854

INTRODUCTION

Founders and Famous Families: Cincinnati traces the interwoven stories of the founding families who made Cincinnati the complex tapestry of industry, art, sport, and pork that it is today. Yes, pork.

Many history books about communities and people of the United States start with a story of how Europeans discovered virgin land, claimed it for their countries, and gave it a name. If the land they discovered had inhabitants, the "discoverers" named them, too. But our story of Cincinnati starts a little differently. For one thing, it wasn't always called "Cincinnati."

More than 400 million years ago, we might have called it "Crinoid City," for a shallow inland sea covered what we would later call Cincinnati. This sea was full of marine animals such as brachiopods, coral, bryozoans, and the tulip-like crinoids or "stone lilies." When these critters died, their calcium-rich shells became part of the fossiliferous limestone in future Cincinnatians' mantels, retaining walls, and garden walkways.

But when it came to actually naming our fair city, some folks in the eighteenth century were a little more forward. Matthias Denman, Israel Ludlow, and Robert Patterson bought 800 acres from John Cleves Symmes, who had been given a charter by the new Continental Congress to settle this area. Symmes had purchased a large section of land (at 66¢ an acre) north of the Ohio River and bordered by the Little and Great Miami rivers, hoping to establish a settlement—thereby making himself wealthy along the way.

Surveyor John Filson—with Denman, Ludlow, and Patterson's help—named their plot of land "Losantiville," which they declared meant "city across from the mouth of the Licking River." "L" was for the Licking River; "os" is Latin for "mouth"; "anti" means "opposite"; and "ville" is French for "town" or "village."

So Losantiville it was—for about a year. Then General Arthur St. Clair, newly named governor of the Northwest Territory, named it "Cincinnati" after the Society of the Cincinnati, of which he was a member. Around Cincinnati even today, however, you can still find remnants of "Losantiville," such as Losantiville Country Club in Pleasant Ridge or Losantiville Avenue in Golf Manor.

But we're getting ahead of ourselves. Let's go back to Cincinnati's geology briefly. We're going to skip ahead from the crinoids of the Paleozoic Era to the Pleistocene Period in the Cenozoic Era. In non-geologic terms, we are talking now about a time approximately 1 million years ago. At this point, there are still no humans. But there are glaciers—the Kansan, the Illinoian, and the Wisconsinan. These three glaciers carved out the valleys and hills that made Cincinnati what it is today, topographically. Prior to that, the main body of water (called the "Teays River" by geologists) flowed northerly, which is why the Licking River flows northerly. The Licking fed the Teays just as the Licking now feeds the Ohio.

The city proper lies in the bottom of a bowl surrounded by the hills that were pushed into shape by these great geological forces of nature. The bowl was also created by the convergence of the Licking, Ohio, Little Miami, and Great Miami rivers. The walls of the bowl, which once protected early settlers, have also served as a natural windbreak—making the Ohio Valley a catch basin for allergens and airborne particulates. Thanks to its hills, Cincinnati has earned one of its other nicknames, "the sinus capital of the world."

And what about those hills? Ask any Cincinnatian how many hills the city has, and he or she will quickly answer "seven!" But if you ask that same friendly Cincinnatian to name those seven hills, you might find your new friend has become a little tongue-tied. Why? Because there are more than just seven hills surrounding the city. Here are a few of the "seven" hills: Clifton Heights, College Hill, Fairmount, Fairview Heights, Mount Adams, Mount Airy, Mount Auburn, Mount Lookout, Mount Echo, Mount Storm, Mount Healthy, Mount Washington, Price Hill, the Vine Street Hill, and Walnut Hills. (The highest of these is Mount Airy, with an elevation of 938 feet above sea level.)

So why *seven* hills? For one possible explanation, we turn to Rome. When General Arthur St. Clair changed the name of the city to Cincinnati, he was naming it for the Society of the Cincinnati. The society honored those who fought during the Revolutionary War and was named for Cincinnatus of ancient Rome—the *original* city of seven hills. So one modern-day theory is that Cincinnatians felt that because Rome had seven hills, so should we.

Another common theory behind the "seven" hills is that the hills closest to the downtown area were the "original" seven hills, only to be later eclipsed by other hills farther out. In fact, in the late nineteenth century, "inclined planes" were built on five of the closest hills. These "inclines" then carried pedestrians and horse cars from downtown Cincinnati to the neighborhoods on the surrounding hills. In this way, the elevated surrounding neighborhoods became much more accessible to Cincinnatians for business, for recreation, or simply for a view of the city from above.

Today, the view from above the city is pretty fantastic. Cincinnati's downtown comprises an eclectic array representing architects and designers from Samuel Hannaford and Frederick Garber to Gyo Obata and Zaha Hadid.

Many people are attracted to Cincinnati for its combination of arts, sports, industry, and state-of-the-art healthcare facilities. And although it is the third-largest city in Ohio, Cincinnati still offers a healthy amount of green spaces with plenty of opportunities to get back to nature. Only a half-hour drive separates the city from forest or farmland. At one point in the 1980s, Cincinnati was even named the greenest city in America.

When I prepared to move here more than three decades ago, I encountered an interesting phenomenon: It seemed as though everyone had either lived here once or knew someone who did. It was as if Cincinnati was everyone's home.

Contrary to a popular saying about visiting versus living somewhere, Cincinnati is a great place to visit *and* live because the city possesses a unique combination of elements.

- down-home hospitality, common to many Midwestern cities
- small-town feel, thanks to all the neighborhoods annexed by Cincinnati
- big-city amenities, such as several universities and professional sports franchises
- cutting-edge healthcare: three hospitals in the top ranks nationally, plus many more highly ranked in specialties ranging from pediatrics to geriatrics
- business leaders: at this writing, 10 Fortune 500 companies and 3 Fortune 500 global companies headquartered here; 15 Fortune 1000 companies and more than 360 Fortune 500 companies with some kind of presence here
- world-renowned fine arts: the second-oldest opera company in the United States, the oldest continuous choral tradition in the western hemisphere (the May Festival Chorus), the fifth-oldest symphony orchestra, the Cincinnati Arts Museum, and much more

In fact, Cincinnatians proclaim their city is one of only a baker's dozen of North American cities that has all the major performance and visual arts disciplines: an opera, a ballet, a symphony, a theatre, and a museum.[1]

A theatre? A museum? Cincinnati has more than five of each.

When I considered whom to include in this book, two things became evident: Cincinnatians don't stay in neat little categories such as business, fine arts, healthcare, education, or politics. The founding families might have made their mark in one area—soap, for example—but they also contributed to the welfare of their fellow Cincinnatians in other arenas (sometimes literally). And Cincinnati's future foundational families are continuing the tradition.

James Norris Gamble, son of Procter & Gamble cofounder James Gamble, donated the funding for a football stadium to the University of Cincinnati in memory of his grandson, James Gamble Nippert (who died as a result of a Thanksgiving Day football game in 1923). Carl Lindner, père, made his early fortune in the dairy world, coming up with the first cash-and-carry dairy store in Cincinnati and naming it United Dairy Farmers. His son, Carl H. Lindner Jr., carried on the UDF tradition but also established and grew many other businesses. Furthermore, he was a great patron of the arts and part-owner of the Cincinnati Reds.

So how did I choose which families to include in this book? After much mulling, I came up with a set of criteria. The founding families in this book did some combination of the following:

- They played an important role in moving Cincinnati forward. For example, John Cleves Symmes got the original charter to settle this area.

- They had several members and/or generations who contributed to Cincinnati's or Cincinnatians' existence. For example, several generations of Longworths and Westheimers contributed to Cincinnati.

---

1 Tom Callinan, "Cincinnati having a special moment for the arts," Op-ed from Cincinnati. com, originally published 8/12/03. Accessed at **http://constellafestival.org/cincinnati-having-a-special-moment-for-the-arts**, 1/8/14, and "Cincinnati USA: A Region of Opportunities," accessed at **http://jobs-ohio.com/images/southwest-region-overview.pdf**, 1/8/14.

- They had a name that modern Cincinnatians would recognize in some way, as in Nippert Stadium, Longworth Hall, or Symmes Township.

- They were or are of national importance. William Howard Taft is perhaps the most famous Taft of his era, having served as both president and chief justice of the United States, but he was just one of many very active Tafts.

I ignored the differences between those people who were born in Cincinnati and those who immigrated here. John Cleves Symmes was born in New York, but he would later get a charter to come here, to what was at that time the last bastion of civilization before the "wild" western frontier. And that's where our story begins.

||||||||||||||||||

Cincinnati Milestones

YEAR	FIRST, LAST, or ONLY
1793	Cincinnati became the first settlement in Ohio to publish a newspaper.
1831	Woodward High School was the first free public school west of the Alleghenies and is the third-oldest high school still operating today.
1835	First airmail, July 4, when a bag of mail was lifted by a hot air balloon.
1843	First observatory was built by public subscription (dedicated by John Quincy Adams, hence the name Mount Adams).
1849	First city in the United States to hold a municipal song festival, which was called a "Saengerfest."
1850	First city in the country to establish a Jewish hospital.
1850	First city in the United States to publish greeting cards—Gibson Greeting Card Company.
1853	First paid municipal fire department with a working steam-powered fire engine *and* a fire pole.
1865	First ambulance service for hospitals—Cincinnati Commercial Hospital.
1867	John Roebling's Covington & Cincinnati Suspension Bridge was the longest suspension bridge and the prototype for the Brooklyn Bridge.

YEAR	FIRST, LAST, or ONLY
1867	Ida Gray was born, destined to be the first African American woman in America to become a dentist; Dr. Gray had a very successful practice in Cincinnati and later moved to Chicago after marrying first James Nelson, then William Rollins. By then known as Dr. Ida N. Rollins, she also became the first African American woman to be a dentist in Chicago.
1869	First city to establish a weather bureau, also the first to issue a weather bulletin.
1869	First professional baseball team—then known as the Cincinnati Red Stockings, now known as the Cincinnati Reds.
1870	First annual Industrial Exposition in America.
1870	First municipal university in the country—Cincinnati College, now the University of Cincinnati.
1875	First Jewish Theological College in the United States—the Hebrew Union College.
1875	First "crowd sourced" matching fundraiser when Reuben Springer offered to finance the building of Music Hall for the May Festival if citizens would also contribute.
1876	From 1876 to 1989, the Reds were given the honor of opening the Opening Day games, as the oldest Major League baseball team; the two exceptions were 1877 and 1966 because of weather.
1880	First and only city to own a railroad—Cincinnati Southern.
1880	First large manufacturing operation to be started and run by a woman, Maria Longworth Nichols Storer's Rookwood Pottery.
1886	The Cincinnati Art Museum opens, the first art museum in its own building west of the Alleghenies.
1890	First standard cantilever truss bridge ever built—Central Bridge (really, the Cincinnati & Newport Bridge)—was completed between Roebling's Covington & Cincinnati suspension bridge and the L&N Bridge; demolished in 1992 and replaced by the Taylor-Southgate Bridge three years later.
1902	First concrete skyscraper—Ingalls Building, 4th & Vine at 15 stories, 210 feet, it remained the world's tallest reinforced concrete structure for two decades.
1902	First grocery store to make its own bread—Kroger.
1905	Daniel Carter Beard founded the Sons of Daniel Boone, later known as the Boy Scouts of America.
1906	First university to offer cooperative education—created by Herman Schneider, dean of engineering at the University of Cincinnati (he later became president of the university).

YEAR	FIRST, LAST, or ONLY
1910	First time the president of the United States throws out the opening day baseball at the Reds game—William Howard Taft, April 14.
1914	Martha (named for Martha Washington), the last passenger pigeon, died at the Cincinnati Zoo and Botanical Garden; she is on display at the Smithsonian Institution in Washington, D. C.
1918	Incus, the last Carolina Parakeet, also died at the Cincinnati Zoo and Botanical Garden, where his body can still be found.
1935	First Major League Baseball game played under the lights—Reds versus the Philadelphia Phillies, May 24 (Reds won, 2–1); they went on to play every National League team at night that year, eight in all. Five hundred miles away, President Franklin D. Roosevelt threw the switch in the White House to light Crosley Field. (Incidentally, the minor leagues had been playing night games since 1930.)
1937	The nation's first interstate electric bus line left Dixie Terminal en route to Northern Kentucky—July 11.
1943	First woman buried in Arlington National Cemetery—Helen "Nellie" (Mrs. William Howard) Taft.
1952	First heart-lung machine, developed at Cincinnati Children's Hospital Medical Center, makes open heart surgery possible.
1954	First licensed educational TV station—WCET-TV.
1957	Children's Hospital researcher Dr. Albert Sabin developed the first oral polio vaccine, which was licensed in 1962. He later also developed vaccines against dengue fever, sand-fly fever, and encephalitis.
1969	Neil Armstrong became the first man to walk on the moon; he later taught in the Aerospace Engineering Department at the University of Cincinnati, the second-oldest aerospace program in the country, which was designed by Orville Wright. Armstrong died in Cincinnati in 2012.

CHAPTER 1

THEY BUILT CINCINNATI

MANY OF THE EARLY PEOPLE WHO LIVED in this area are known to us now as Mound Builders. By the end of the seventeenth century, however, those of the Mound Builder culture had disappeared from this area of southwest Ohio. (The work of the Mound Builders closest to Cincinnati, of the Fort Ancient Culture, can best be seen at Serpent Mound in Adams County.) About 100 years went by with no other groups filling the void. Previously farmed fields lay fallow. So at the beginning of the 1700s, southwest Ohio was sparsely populated.

Then, having been driven out of New York, the Iroquois entered Ohio and spread quickly throughout the state, fighting other tribes and completely wiping out some, like the Erie, along the way. In their attempts to claim so much land, however, the Iroquois spread themselves too thin and thus left themselves vulnerable to attack from many sides by others.

The Miami tribes came in from the west and established a stronghold on that side of the state, eventually giving their name to many landmarks that still exist today, such as Miami University. Three rivers, in fact, bear variations of the Miami name: the Great Miami to the west of Cincinnati, the Little Miami to the east, and the Maumee to the north.

From the Great Lakes came the Wyandot Hurons, Ottawas, Potawatomies, and Chippewas (Ojibwes). The Shawnee traveled along the Scioto River from the east, as did the Delaware tribe, who came from Pennsylvania and settled in central Ohio. Fort Ancient itself, in Warren County just northeast of Cincinnati, had become home to other tribes. No one tribe of native people had a clear hold on Southwestern Ohio.

At the same time that these Native American forces were fighting each other for the land, the British and French had also discovered Ohio and battled for control of the region. As of July 4, 1776, all this was taking place in a country that we now think of as the United States of America. But back then this area was better described as being an utter state of chaos.

In 1780, an expedition of soldiers was launched against the Native Americans. George Rogers Clark led a contingent of more than a thousand men with the goal of driving the Indians back and teaching them a lesson for recent attacks on settlers in Kentucky and Ohio. Official Ohio statistics papers published by the Secretary of State in the late 1800s contain a description, written by a Mr. Isaac Smucker, of the construction of two blockhouses directly across from the mouth of the Licking River on August 1, 1780. By Clark's command, these blockhouses were to be guarded for 14 days until his return and then abandoned. Eventually, they were destroyed with no evidence left of their exact location.

Other people were floating into Losantiville at the same time. William Lytle brought his family down the Ohio from Pennsylvania in 1780. Along with his wife, the former Mary Steele, he brought their family of several children. Lytle's river party consisted of a fleet of flatboats including immigrants from England, Ireland, and Scotland. (Many years later, William's great-grandson, then-Colonel William Haines Lytle, commented on the mostly Irish Cincinnati regiment during the Civil War, saying, "There is not a man in these ranks who will not shed his heart's blood like water beneath these colors."[1])

As the flotilla of flatboats neared its objective, the group noticed a large band of Native Americans encamped at the mouth of the Licking River. They attempted to run them off. Their efforts were less than successful, however, as several natives escaped and several of their attackers fled as well. The group continued floating down to Louisville.

The Lytles didn't stay there, though. Lytle's son, another William Lytle, and his wife—the former Eliza Stahl—returned to Ohio and founded the community of Williamsburg, eventually returning to Cincinnati. This William Lytle purchased 8 acres of land in what later became known as "Lytle Square" in downtown Cincinnati's neighborhood of Fourth, Lawrence, and Third Streets, neighbors of the Tafts and Longworths.

William Lytle fought in the War of 1812 and reached the rank of General. Service to the country ran in the Lytle family. General Lytle's son Robert Todd Lytle served one term in the United States House of Representatives and was known for his great oration skills. Robert Todd Lytle's only son, William Haines Lytle, fought in both the Mexican-American and Civil Wars, was wounded twice and taken prisoner twice, and reached the rank of Brigadier General. Besides being a soldier, however, William Haines Lytle was also known for his writing—especially his poetry. His "Antony and Cleopatra" was a staple for schoolchildren to memorize as recently as the 1940s.

At the Civil War Battle of Chickamauga near Chattanooga in 1863, when the fatal bullet hit him (even injuring his horse), Lytle died within minutes. Brigadier General William Haines Lytle died on September 20, 1863, at the age of 37. His poetry was so admired

---

1 "Ohio's Immigrant Soldiers in the Civil War," Aroh Miller, 10/28/13. Accessed at **http:// www.ohiocivilwar150.org/2013/10/ohios-immigrant-soldiers-in-the-civil-war**, 1/8/14.

and he was so respected by Northerners and Southerners alike that Confederate soldiers guarded his body until Lytle's own troops could retrieve him. His body was then allowed to be transported home to Cincinnati—a very unusual occurrence during the Civil War. He is buried in Spring Grove Cemetery.

The mansion that General William Lytle had built in the early 1800s was—according to his will—to remain in the Lytle family in perpetuity. William Haines Lytle had been born there in 1826. In 1834, the Lytles had entertained President Andrew Jackson there during his only visit to Cincinnati. Starting in 1900, the city decided it wanted the land for a park. After time, the mansion needed repairs. One of the leading ladies of Cincinnati, Mary Emery, offered to step in and pay for the repairs, but the city council refused to allow it. Under continued pressure from the crooked administration of "Boss" Cox, the family buckled and sold the land and the mansion to the city. The mansion was razed and Lytle Park was created. When the construction of I-71 threatened the park, the Lytle Tunnel was built so that the park would not be disturbed.

The Lytle family had arrived seven years before the signing of the ordinance to settle the Northwest Territory. Theirs was one of the first permanent homes constructed in Cincinnati.

Captain Benjamin Stites arrived in 1786. While helping settlers chase down stolen horses, he traveled up the Little Miami Valley about as far north as the modern-day Yellow Springs/Xenia area. After giving up the stolen horse chase, Stites and the rest of the posse crossed the Little Miami and travelled west to its sister river, the Great Miami, probably just above where Dayton is today. They followed the Great Miami back down to the Ohio, near the modern-day border with Indiana.

Although they came back without the stolen horses, Stites had gained something else: a look at the land he wanted to settle, between the two Miami Rivers. Upon returning to New Jersey, Stites heard that John Cleves Symmes, chief justice of the state of New Jersey,

Baby, I'm for Real

Picture Cincinnati in the eighteenth century. Many parts of town that we consider Cincinnati now were known by different names back then and were considered separate settlements. Factor in the lack of hospitals and doctors, with most babies born at home with the assistance of family members or midwives—and no Internet for making announcements. That adds up to a lot of confusion when trying to identify notable births. Many people have considered it important to know who the first white baby was. Given that the majority of the first settlers here were of Western European ancestry, it is almost understandable that the historical focus has been on who the first white baby was. Today, though, who the first white baby born in Cincinnati was seems like a moot point, given that thousands of Native American babies were born before the first white baby. We have no record of them. We also have no record of who the first African-American, Asian-American or Hispanic babies were. But we have lots of records—or "opinions" might be more accurate in some cases—about the first white baby.

William Moody, born March 17, 1790, was widely acknowledged during his lifetime as being the first white child born in Losantiville. He was born in a log cabin near the corner of Fourth and Main Streets. Even during his lifetime, Moody was referred to as the first white baby born in the city. He died in 1879; at his death he was acknowledged by the mayor as he who had been regarded as the first white child born when the town numbered only 200 residents.

"... [This] child grew to manhood and lived long enough to see Cincinnati become the Queen City of the West, teeming with an active, energetic, thrifty population of over three hundred thousand people," the mayor said. "How hard it is to realize the fact that such wonderful, marvelous changes could take place within the lifetime of a single citizen."

One of the most interesting stories is told in *My First 70 Years* by "Mrs. George Black, F.R.G.S., MP for the Yukon, as told to Elizabeth Bailey Price. "Mrs. George Black was born Martha Louise Owens on February 27, 1866. (Besides the challenges mentioned earlier, Mrs. Black's accounts highlight a difficulty well known to genealogists: women "disappear" when they marry and assume their husbands' names, thus making it difficult to track them through history.) Mrs. Black adds a personal twist to her tale:

"Mother [Susie B. Owens] was the daughter of John W. Owens, owner of a large plantation and several Ohio River packets—a member of the family [that] founded Owensville, Kentucky [sic], where she was born. Her mother was Mary Ludlow Cummins, of Ohio, after whom Cumminsville was named. Her [Susie's] grandmothers, Jeanette Cummins and Susan Ludlow, were accredited to be the mothers of the first white boy and first white girl born in Cincinnati. For years portraits of these grandmothers, bequeathed by Grandfather Owens to the Young Men's Mercantile Library Association, hung in the Cincinnati City Hall."

Other records substantiate a Ludlow being the first baby, but without agreement on the name. Sheriff John Ludlow, whose mother's name was Catherine Cooper, married his first cousin—also named Catherine Cooper. They had five children together, the youngest of whom was Cooper Ludlow, who was recorded as being born on June 11, 1783, in "Cincinnati." If this is true, then he was the first white (male) child and beat William Moody by seven years. However, it is said that John Ludlow came to Ohio by himself in 1786 but did not bring his family here until 1789, so it is unlikely that this record is correct.

But wait! There's more! Ludlow's first wife died in 1783, after which he remarried. His second wife was Susan Demun (or DeMun, in some documents), with whom he had seven more children. Their first, William, is also recorded as having been born in Cincinnati, but as he was born in 1785 it is unlikely that he was born in Ohio. His first younger sister Mary, however, was born in November 1791, and therefore could be the first white girl baby to whom Mrs. Black referred: the daughter of Susan (and John) Ludlow. Dr. Daniel Drake described Cincinnati as a village of infants. He believed that David Cummins was the first white child born in what became known as the neighborhood of Cumminsville. However, this part of Cincinnati is more than six miles from downtown; back then it was not considered part of Losantiville. Drake admitted that he wasn't even certain of Cummins' birth date. However, if Drake was correct, then his account would corroborate the other half of Mrs. Black's story: David Cummins could be the son of Jeanette Cummins, and therefore the first white baby boy.

Historian Charles Cist said in 1845 that he couldn't find anyone older than David R. Kemper, born on May 17, 1793, on Sycamore Street. At that point, however, even William Moody was already more than three years old. Daniel Gano, born May 27 or 29, 1794, in a house at Front and Lawrence Streets, eventually became the clerk of the Court of Common Pleas and Supreme Court, as well as the clerk of the Superior Court. Common Pleas Court Judge A. G. W. Carter said of Maj. Gano, "He was, I believe, among the first white children, if not the very first white child born in the city of Cincinnati." Gano's birth, though, had been preceded by Moody's by four years. According to the *History of the Early Settlers of Sangamon County, Illinois: Centennial Record,* by John Carroll Power and Sarah A. Harris Power, Martha Cutter was the first white child born in Cincinnati. However, recorded dates of her birth range from 1786 to 1790. Perhaps no one will ever know who truly was the first white child born in Cincinnati. Other children preceded that first white one; other children followed. As many more settlers moved into Cincinnati, babies were bound to follow and follow they still do. In the twenty-first century, with our collection of many excellent hospitals, people come from the surrounding communities to have their babies in Cincinnati. The babies born each year now number in the thousands, but they don't all live here. We'll leave that to future historians to sort out.

was purchasing land under a charter for the new Northwest Territory. Stites, Matthias Denman, and about 60 others then joined Symmes as he prepared for coming here in 1788.

Meanwhile, the newly named Congress of the Confederation had convened in New York City. On July 13, 1787, they had passed what became known as the Northwest Ordinance, but was formally titled "An Ordinance for the Government of the Territory of the United States, North-west of the Ohio River." This document dispensed with any previous claims to lands west of Pennsylvania and north of the Ohio River and put all land under federal control. The Northwest Ordinance addressed personal freedoms that the Constitution of the United States (written the same year) didn't cover. It also set down the requirements for a territory to become a state.

John Cleves Symmes was given a charter in 1788 to buy and settle about 2 million acres of this Northwest Territory between the Little and Great Miami Rivers. This charter was the result of work that Symmes had begun in 1787 after his own visit to the Ohio River Valley. Symmes formed a land company, counting among its membership such now-familiar names as Elias Boudinot and Jonathan Dayton. Symmes began advertising land lots available for purchase, suitable for log cabins. Thus, Judge Symmes set out from the east to create the new west.

Symmes's party stopped when they reached a place called Limestone (now known as Maysville, near the home of Rosemary, Nick, George, and all the other Clooneys). From there, the group ran numerous sorties (from the French word *sortir*, which means "to leave" or "to go out") to get familiar with the area. Symmes originally wanted *all* of the land between the two Miamis, but ended up settling on a little more than 300,000 acres. Stites chose the area where the Little Miami runs into the Ohio River on the east side of Cincinnati, naming his settlement "Columbia." He bought 10,000 acres altogether along the Ohio and the Little Miami.

Cincinnatians nowadays will recognize this area as Columbia-Tusculum, through which Columbia Parkway runs, hugging the border between some of Cincinnati's hills and the shore of the Ohio. Columbia was incorporated on November 18, 1788.

Today if you take Columbia Parkway in from the east to downtown Cincinnati, you're treated to breathtaking views of the Cincinnati skyline as well as Kentucky and the Ohio River itself. Your passengers, if unaccustomed to the proximity of the retaining wall to the north and the water to the south, might refer to the drive as a white-knuckle flight. There's a thin line between breathtaking and heart-stopping.

Robert Patterson and Matthias Denman chose a more central location to establish their roots. Denman had purchased an 800-acre piece of land right at a dip in the Ohio across from the mouth of the Licking River. In a way that would make Nat King Cole proud, Surveyor John Filson, Denman, Patterson, and Chief Surveyor Israel Ludlow came up with a name for their settlement: "Losantiville." (Today the name "Losantiville" can be found as a street, a school, and even a country club in Cincinnati.) Losantiville was incorporated on December 28, 1788, as the city across from the mouth of the Licking River.

Over the years, many people have been credited with creating the fanciful name, but it was most likely John Filson's idea. Besides being a surveyor, he had also been a schoolmaster and a writer. His facility with words can be seen in his description of Kentucky: "When I visited Kentucky I found it so far to exceed my expectations, though great that I concluded it was a pity that the world has not adequate information of it. I conceived that a proper description of it was an object highly interesting to the United States, and, therefore, incredible as it may appear to some I must declare that this performance is not published from lucrative motives, but solely to inform the world of the happy climate and plentiful soul of this favored region."[2]

---

2 Henry A. Ford, Kate B. Ford, *History of Cincinnati, Ohio, with Illustrations and Biographical Sketches.* (Cleveland: L. A. Williams & Co. 1881), 28.

William Henry Venable (named for William Henry Harrison) was a revered nineteenth-century historian, poet, and teacher at Walnut Hills High School. Venable felt that John Filson did not receive enough credit for the naming of Losantiville, so he wrote a ballad for Filson. Here's the beginning:

> *John Filson was a pedagogue—*
> *A pioneer was he,*
> *I know not what his nation was*
> *Nor what his pedigree . . . .*
> *John Filson from three languages*
> *With pedant skill did frame*
> *The novel word Losantiville*
> *To be the new town's name . . . .*

Surveyor Israel Ludlow divided Losantiville into two different types of lots: half-acre lots in the downtown area and 4-acre parcels up from the river. Denman, Patterson, and Ludlow then gave one of each type of lot to the 30 families who now populated Losantiville.

Israel Ludlow married Charlotte Chambers, of Chambersburg, Pennsylvania, with whom he had four children. (His granddaughter, Sarah Bella "Belle" Dunlop Ludlow, became the third wife of Salmon P. Chase—governor of Ohio, secretary of the Treasury under President Lincoln, and one-time Republican presidential candidate.) Israel's half-brother, John Ludlow, also settled in Losantiville, becoming its first sheriff. Israel built a two-room house for John at Front and Main Streets, close to where Great American Ballpark is now.

Matthias Denman eventually married a daughter of the Baldwin family. Modern-day Cincinnatians will recognize the Baldwin name as one of the many piano dynasties to spring from the city.

From their encampment in Limestone (aka Maysville) John Cleves Symmes and his party would make themselves familiar with the surrounding territory through small trips known as sorties. Leaving Limestone on one sortie, Symmes retraced his earlier visit downriver toward modern-day Louisville.

On the trip, surveyor Filson and some Kentuckians were reprimanded by Symmes for shooting at local tribesman. Symmes returned to Limestone, but Filson and the other Kentuckians quit in disgust. Filson left the group and disappeared. He was presumed to have been killed by Native Americans.

Professor Venable sang of that, too:

> *. . . Deep in the wild and solemn woods,*
> *Unknown to white man's track*
> *John Filson went one autumn day*
> *But nevermore came back. . . .*
> *And may my simple ballad be*
> *A monument to save*
> *His name from blank oblivion*
> *Who never had a grave.*

Symmes had planned to settle at the mouth of the Great Miami, but after noting the flooding problems encountered by the settlers in Columbia, he chose a site about 5 miles to the east, instead. He called his settlement "North Bend" or "Great Bend," for the sudden northward bend in the Ohio River. Symmes's North Bend was settled on February 2, 1789.

North Bend shares a claim to fame with Quincy (pronounced "QUIN-zee"), Massachusetts. To date, they're the only two cities that can boast of being home to two U.S. presidents (unless you count Midland, Texas, where George Herbert Walker Bush moved after college, before starting his family). Quincy, population

William Henry Harrison, originally trained as a medic, became general over Fort Washington and the son-in-law of John Cleves Symmes.

Credit: Library of Congress, public domain

92,271 as of the 2010 U.S. Census, was home to John Adams and John Quincy Adams. (The town and he were both named after his maternal grandfather.) North Bend, population 4,004 as of the 2010 U.S. Census, was the birthplace of Benjamin Harrison and the resting place of William Henry Harrison.

The original Fort Washington (before it became a "Way" for busy drivers during rush hour) was built by order of General Josiah Harmar. Sitting just east of what is now the intersection of Third and Broadway, it was established as a defense against the British and the Native Americans. The fort was constructed during most of 1789 on what was considered to be the northeastern edge of

The earliest homes were lean-tos and log cabins

Losantiville. The large log structure contained barracks as well as storage and utility buildings. When General Harmar and 300 troops arrived on December 29, 1789, to inhabit the fort, the entire village of Losantiville welcomed them: all 11 families and 24 single men.

The earliest homes were lean-tos and log cabins, which were about 16 to 20 feet long and 12 to 16 feet wide. Most were one-floor homes, with an occasional loft. Later homes were frame houses of wood or brick, some two-storied. Wealthier homeowners tended to have houses that were larger, of more complex materials, and with more furnishings that were often brought with them from the east. Some of the single men made their homes in flatboats down by the river.

Arthur St. Clair arrived in January to assume his new role as governor of the Northwest Territory, but he didn't care for the name Losantiville. At a banquet given in his honor on January 4, 1790, he announced that the town would now be known as Cincinnati, after the Society of Cincinnati, of which he was a member.

In a letter dated 1791, John Cleves Symmes requested a New Jersey friend to ask the "literati" of New Jersey whether they thought "Cincinnat*i*" or "Cincinnat*a*" was more proper. "I think the name of a town should terminate in the feminine gender," he wrote. For a while he used both. Perhaps this explains why, to this day, longtime Cincinnati residents, those whose families have lived here for generations, as well as those who live in Southern Ohio in general, tend to still refer to Cincinnati as "Cincinnata."

One might get the idea that the top concern was the name of the settlement, but despite the presence of many settlers and the fort itself, all was not well in the new village. The white settlers still felt threatened by the Native American tribes in the area. So General Harmar led 320 "regulars" and more than 1,000 recruits up the Miami Valley as far as the Maumee River. He was not successful, though; he only succeeded in losing more than 200 men and riling up the native peoples he had been fighting.

General Arthur St. Clair led the next expedition himself, in March 1791, to fight back the Indian presence, with results similar to Harmar's—but even worse. Amassing a force of regulars, recruits, and Kentucky militia that totaled almost 2,000 men (plus another 200 "camp followers" of wives, cooks, seamstresses, and prostitutes), St. Clair set off to take on the entire American Indian Confederacy made up of fighters of the Miami, Shawnee, Potawatomi, and Delaware tribes.

By the time the fighting was over, only about 50 of St. Clair's men survived—less than 3 percent of the original force. Proportionally speaking, it was one of the worst routs in U.S. military history. One-quarter of the entire U.S. Army was lost. President George Washington demanded St. Clair's resignation—and got it.

Finally a successful attempt was led by General "Mad Anthony" Wayne in the summer of 1794. (He earned this nickname from his crazy exploits and his practice of taking risks.) His plan focused on multiple fronts, specifically what is termed "battle and belly": he starved the Native American Indians out, destroyed their crops, and then attacked. The final victory for the military came about 200 miles northeast of Cincinnati at Fallen Timbers, in what is now known as the city of Maumee, southwest of modern-day Toledo.

The battle was more decisive but far less deadly than St. Clair's futile campaign had been. Fewer than 100 people died on each side. Yet when it was over, the tribes ceded their rights to the land in the Northwest Territory.

The resultant Treaty of Greenville was signed on August 3, 1795, by General Wayne as well as the leaders of a dozen major Native American tribes: the Wyandots, Delawares, Shawnees, Ottawas, Chippewas (Ojibwes), Potawotamis, Miamis, and a handful of smaller tribes. The Native Americans agreed to yield certain lands in exchange for money and goods—$1,000 to the major tribes and $500 to the smaller groups.

The U.S. government also agreed to give up certain lands in return, declaring that "the Indian tribes who have a right to those lands, are quietly to enjoy them, hunting, planting, and dwelling thereon so long as they please, without any molestation from the United States; but when those tribes, or any of them, shall be disposed to sell their lands, or any part of them, they are to be sold only to the United States; and until such sale, the United States will protect all the said Indian tribes in the quiet enjoyment of their lands against all citizens of the United States, and against all other white persons who intrude upon the same. And the said Indian tribes again acknowledge themselves to be under the protection of the said United States and no other power whatever."

General Wayne was especially impressed with a certain Lieutenant William Henry Harrison's bravery at the Battle of the Fallen Timbers, writing this commendation: "I must add the name of my faithful and gallant Aide-de-camp . . . Lieutenant Harrison, who . . . rendered the most essential service by communicating my

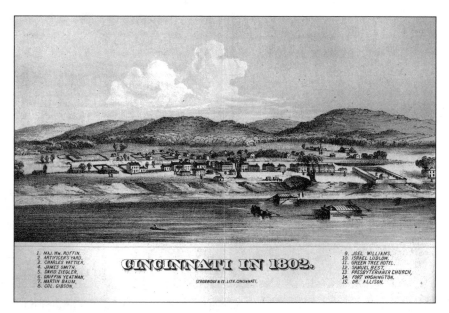

1. MAJ. Wm. RUFFIN.
2. ARTIFICER'S YARD.
3. CHARLES VATTIER.
4. JAMES SMITH.
5. DAVID ZIEGLER.
6. GRIFFIN YEATMAN.
7. MARTIN BAUM.
8. COL. GIBSON.

CINCINNATI IN 1802.

STROBRIDGE & CO. LITH. CINCINNATI.

9. JOEL WILLIAMS.
10. ISRAEL LUDLOW.
11. GREEN TREE HOTEL.
12. SAMUEL BEST.
13. PRESBYTERIANER CHURCH.
14. FORT WASHINGTON.
15. DR. ALLISON.

Cincinnati was incorporated as a village in 1802, with a population of about 1,000 people. Fort Washington is on the right, with homes of prominent citizens labeled.

Credit: From *The Queen City in 1869* by George E. Stevens, Library of Congress

orders in every direction. . . . [his] conduct and bravery exciting the troops to press for victory." Before becoming the ninth president of the United States, William Henry Harrison—originally trained as a medic of sorts—would become commander of Fort Washington at Wayne's death.

Someone else was also impressed by the young lieutenant: Harrison would also become John Cleves Symmes's son-in-law by marrying Anna Tuthill Symmes in 1795. Symmes objected to the marriage, so they eloped. At the end of John Cleves Symmes's life, he wound up "land poor" and in poor health. Someone set fire to his house in Cincinnati and he lost everything he owned, so he moved in with his daughter and son-in-law and there spent his last days. He died from an oral cancer on February 26, 1814.

The central site for Fort Washington had been chosen because of the frequent flooding of Columbia and North Bend. It became

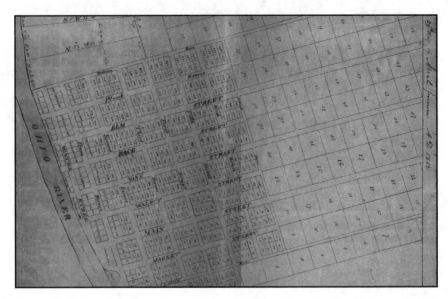

Several of the original north-south streets still exist today (so the mnemonic then would just be "Men Will Very Rarely Eat Pork"). The east-west streets up to Fourth Street were frequently flooded.

Credit: From "Record of the distribution and sale of lots in the town of Losantiville 1789" by Robert Clarke, including surveyor Israel Ludlow's list of which settler bought each plot. Library of Congress, public domain

apparent that of the three settlements, Losantiville was the best location in relation to the Ohio River. Although the Ohio of the 1790s is nothing like today's river, it still presented difficulties to those who tried to live by its side.

Residents in both Columbia and North Bend were subjected to frequent flooding—but not those living in Cincinnati. Sure, the streets closer to the river might have gotten wet occasionally, but for the most part they were spared. Besides the smaller river size, flooding was also naturally prevented by the sloped bank topping out in a natural shelf at what we now call Fourth Street. Consequently, many settlers from Columbia and North Bend moved inward to Cincinnati, thus making it the biggest settlement. If not for the temperamental Ohio, this book might have been about the founding families of North Bend!

The dawning of the nineteenth century on Cincinnati began its shift from frontier town with an army fort at its foundation to industrial center of commerce, trade, and traffic. Just shy of 15,000 people lived in Hamilton County in 1800. Families began to settle and grow in Cincinnati, which became incorporated as a village in 1802. An act in 1802 also defined village officials, their powers, and duties. A village recorder, assessor, tax collector, and marshal and a council of seven trustees were to be elected by popular vote. Cincinnati counted its population at about 1,000—still mostly men—when Fort Washington finally closed in 1803. Cincinnati was no longer just a military outpost; it was a real village.

Changes were going on in the whole region, too. In 1803, people across Ohio celebrated as it officially became a state on March 1, with Edward Tiffin as the first governor. The General Assembly elected the state's first two United States senators, John Smith and Thomas Worthington, who were sworn in on October 17, when the newly elected eighth Congress first convened.

Modern-day Cincinnatians will recognize the name of Ohio's first representative elected to Congress, Jeremiah Morrow, as his eponymous bridge spans the Little Miami River gorge on Interstate 71. Since 1965, many drivers have gripped their steering wheels more tightly, while braver souls have wished the guardrails allowed a better view of the Little Miami, Ohio's first National Scenic River, gurgling 239 feet below. The Little Miami runs south, joining the Ohio River east of Cincinnati.

A major fire early in 1803 became the impetus for one of Cincinnati's firsts: the creation of the first volunteer fire department in the nation. Cincinnati's Union Fire Company became the first-ever volunteer fire department, in response to concern from citizens whose homes were built from log, frame, and brick. Cincinnati leads the nation in other fire firsts, too: the first full-time paid fire department, the first steam-run fire engine, and the first fire pole.

The Night Watch began by village ordinance on March 29, 1803. All village males over the age of 21 were divided into groups of

12. From each group one young man was chosen as a captain. Two groups served at a time: one for the east side, one for the west. (It is not known if the divider then was Vine Street, the simple street that is the major divider today between Cincinnati's East and West sides and the subject of many good-natured battles.)

The Night Watchmen carried lanterns and large rattles, with which they were to sound an alarm if they saw any "persons they may detect during the night in any felonious act, or any person or persons who are behaving in the streets in a noisy, riotous manner." They didn't wear uniforms or even badges. By 1818 a fund had been established to pay the Night Watchmen so that more professional watchmen could be garnered. The pay of $1 per man per night helped establish a Guard that included a captain and six watchmen whose duties now included arresting rowdy tavern patrons if they disturbed the peace and trimming and lighting the street lamps.

Finally Cincinnati had begun to resemble a town or a destination, instead of just being the beginning of the western frontier. Cincinnati was incorporated as a city in 1819, with a population of about 10,000 and Isaac Burnet as mayor. The new city was quartered into four "wards" by the intersection of Third and Main streets.

The city directory depicts the valiant effort made by John Piatt in building 28 three-story brick houses from 1813 to 1819, as well as 25 frame houses, to provide homes for the large numbers of immigrants. However, the directory was less than effusive in describing the aesthetic of these homes:

> The houses, generally, are rather neat and convenient than splendid, most of those that have been built within the last five or six years, have been constructed of brick, and by far the greater portion of them are two or three stories in height. One prevailing trait, displayed in almost all the houses in town, is a want of architectural taste and skill. All the public buildings, except the Cincinnati banking house, exemplify the above remark. One or two good architects would unquestionably meet here with excellent encouragement.

Unfortunately, Samuel Hannaford didn't arrive from England until 1844, and didn't design his first building for another 22 years, because when he arrived in the United States he was just a boy of 9 years. But once he started designing buildings, he didn't stop until more than 300 buildings later.

Hannaford emigrated with his parents and siblings from England, where he had been born in 1835. He grew up in the Westside neighborhood of Cheviot. His first wife was Phoebe Statham of Cheviot. They moved their family to a home that Samuel built in Winton Place, where Phoebe died from typhoid in 1871. Samuel remarried, choosing Anna Belle Hand, who died in 1883. Hannaford's third wife was Ada Louise Moore. (Samuel's son Charles married Ada's sister Agnes, so his sister-in-law was also his daughter-in-law.) Ada Moore Hannaford outlived her husband, dying in 1941 at the age of 82.

The Workhouse was Hannaford's first building, begun in 1866 and completed in 1869 for more than $470,000. It was demolished in 1991 for its "cruel and inhumane" conditions, but not before several movies were shot there, including *Lock Up*, starring Sylvester Stallone, and *An Innocent Man*, starring Tom Selleck. A. G. Moore, superintendent of Cincinnati Water Works, was looking for a unique design for the building to house the valve works of the Eden Park reservoir. Luckily, he was Samuel Hannaford's brother-in-law. The result, the "Elsinore Tower," designed by Hannaford & Sons, was based on a stage set for Shakespeare's "Hamlet."

The Alms and Doepke department store, built by Samuel Hannaford, can be seen reflected in the Miami & Erie Canal. The building still stands but is the home of shops and government offices on what is now Central Parkway.

Credit: Library of Congress, public domain

One of Hannaford's buildings that still stands was built in 1878 when the Alms and Doepke department store relocated to the far side of the Miami & Erie Canal (now Central Parkway) at Main Street. The store closed in 1955, but the building is now occupied by shops and government offices. The last building that

Samuel Hannaford was directly involved in was Twin Towers (or "the Methodist Home for the Aged"), which was built in 1902.

Samuel Hannaford had many business partners over the years. He started out alone, but found that finances necessitated taking on a partner. From 1858 to 1870 that partner was Edward Anderson. After that he worked alone for a while again, then partnered with Edwin Procter (son of P&G founder William Procter) for two years. Two of Hannaford's sons, Harvey and Charles, had become draftsmen by the late 1870s, so in 1887 they entered their father's business. Hannaford & Sons continued on after their father's death, designing many outstanding buildings. (A list of Hannaford's creations is included in an appendix to this book.)

The origins of Cincinnati's families of the early nineteenth century comprised a mixture of sources; of the 2,400-some adult residents, fewer than 50 had actually been born in Ohio. Of course, the majority of Cincinnati's citizens had arrived from eastern states, especially Pennsylvania, New Jersey, New York, and Massachusetts. Nevertheless, one or two actually were from Michigan and Indiana. However, more than 20 percent of the residents of Cincinnati came from overseas. Ten percent of Cincinnati's citizens were from England, with slightly fewer from Ireland. Only about 50 Germans lived in Cincinnati as of 1825. It is difficult now, given Cincinnati's reputation, to imagine a time when pockets of Cincinnati were not known as Kleindeutschland or Little Germany, tucked away in Over-the-Rhine!

On the Ohio, keelboats and flatboats had been the best modes for transporting goods from the eighteenth to the nineteenth century.

As you would expect from their name, flatboats were boxy and flat. They could be up to 100 feet long and were very difficult to steer. They carried goods downstream but could not go back upriver. At the end of their journey—wherever that might be—they were usually dismantled, with the wood salvaged for other uses, such as new homes for the boatsmen themselves. Finally tents and lean-tos were replaced with more-permanent housing made of wood. Otherwise,

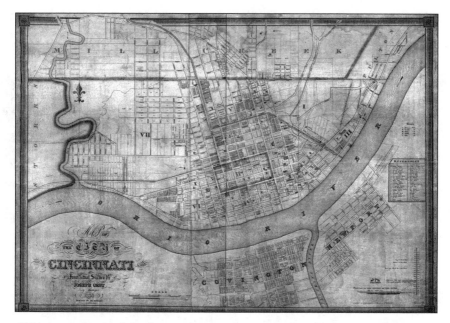

Water was king of the Queen City in the 1830s. Besides the Ohio River, this map depicts the Miami & Erie Canal, which comes in from the northwest and dumps into the Ohio on the east, as well as the Mill Creek on the west and the Licking River—which flows north, unlike most rivers in the United States.

Credit: Library of Congress, public domain

the men from the boats often walked back to Pittsburgh to catch another boat down the Ohio.

Compared to flatboats, keelboats were smaller and shallower boats that also drifted with the current. Between 50 and 80 feet long and about 15 feet wide, the boats did have a keel—but not much of one. Keelboats were more controllable than flatboats, but only in the way a wild horse might be more controllable than a wild bull. Neither one was exactly a pleasure boat.

After riding the current downstream, the men working the boat would then "pole" the boat back upstream by sticking great metal-tipped poles in the river bottom and walking the length of the boat. They might also use rope winches to pull the boat back upstream; this was called "cordelling."

"View of Cincinnati," by J. W. Winder, shows the heavy steamboat traffic in 1866. The suspension bridge, under construction here, opened to pedestrian traffic on December 1 of that year.

Credit: Library of Congress

It was difficult, dangerous work. Besides the physical labor involved, the crew always had to be prepared for threats from the banks. They never knew what kind of reception they would get when or if they pulled ashore. Many different types of people lived along the Ohio: Native Americans as well as white trappers and settlers. A boat and its crew might represent some visitors and welcome conversation, or it might represent unsuspecting victims to be jumped and robbed of their goods.

The round trip from Pittsburgh to Cincinnati and back took about two months. To go downstream all the way from Pittsburgh to New Orleans took only about a month and a half, but the return trip upriver took four months. Two or three round trips per growing season was the norm for the keelboats.

At the turn of the nineteenth century, about 50 keelboats still worked the Ohio. By the end of the first decade, that number had grown threefold—but the keelboat was about to meet some stiff competition in the form of the steamboat. The first steamboat down the Ohio was the brainchild of none other than Nicholas Isaac Roosevelt. (Nicholas's uncle—his father's brother—was President

Theodore Roosevelt's grandfather.) Nicholas Roosevelt was sure that the future of the Ohio River lay in steamboats, so he contacted Robert Fulton about steaming down the Ohio. Fulton was working on a similar idea. They agreed to join their energy and resources: they christened their boat the *New Orleans*.

In 1811, over objections from family and friends, Nicholas Roosevelt and Lydia Latrobe Roosevelt, his wife of two years—and pregnant with their second child at the time—cruised down-river, stopping to disembark in Cincinnati on their 981-mile trip to New Orleans. Their stop in Cincinnati was noted in the newspaper: "Same day—THE STEAMBOAT, lately built at Pittsburgh passed this town at five o'clock in the afternoon in fine style going at the rate of about ten or twelve miles an hour."

Despite the underwhelming newspaper coverage, it was a joyous journey, with much fanfare from those on the banks as well as those on board. Halley's Comet soared overhead, giving the passengers and crew much enjoyment as they viewed it from their moving observatory.

However, the voyage was not exactly a pleasure cruise, either. The Ohio River varied greatly in width and depth in those days before the dams and locks were built. (During the summer in Cincinnati, one could often walk from Kentucky to Ohio without getting com-pletely wet when the water was low.) In some cases, only inches separated the hull of the *New Orleans* from the river bottom. Then, complicating matters further, Mrs. Roosevelt gave birth during the

Who Was Mike Fink?

Many locals know the name of "Mike Fink" as a floating restaurant that could be found anchored in Covington, Kentucky. Listed on the National Register of Historic Places, it occupied a place in the hearts of Cincinnatians and Northern Kentuckians for many years.

But who was Mike Fink? He was probably the most famous keelboat "captain," partially thanks to actor Jeff York's cleaned-up version of him that appeared in Walt Disney television shows and movies (opposite Fess Parker's Davy Crockett). In truth, Mike Fink was a bear of a man, given to large living and larger transgressions that made him a legend among those who worked the keelboats. He was born around 1770 near Pittsburgh and he was a friend of Davy Crockett; that much is true. He was said to have a cabin on the Cumberland River in Kentucky where the lovely Mrs. Fink often waited for her Mike to come home. It makes a nice story, anyway. By 1785 Mike Fink was one of the biggest names on the Ohio and Mississippi keelboats.

By the 1800s, Mike Fink owned two keelboats, which he ran out of Wheeling, West Virginia. In 1822, he was hired to navigate the Missouri River (alongside another legend, Jedediah Smith) up to Montana. Just as he had been a legendary boatman, he was about to become a legendary mountain man, opening up the west and establishing a fur trading post in Montana. So Mike Fink left the Ohio Valley. But he was not long for this world, either. In 1823 a disagreement between him and two other trappers grew violent. Mike Fink was killed, but his legend lived on.

trip. A son joined those onboard, including their little daughter, maids, a waiter, a cook, and a Newfoundland puppy named Tiger.

But shallow water and childbirth were known about ahead of time, to some extent, and could be planned for. One event could not: the 1811 New Madrid earthquake. Its tremors shook the banks as well as the ground under the river, with the ensuing rough waters causing many of the crew and passengers to suffer from seasickness. Tiger's sensitivity to the vibrations kept him upset, requiring frequent comforting by Mrs. Roosevelt.

Many of the native peoples, already frightened by the strange comet in the sky, felt the movement of the ground accompanied by the sight of a noisy water vessel belching steam with a wheel on its side, and concluded that the boat had caused the other events. They ran when approached by the crew of the boat—afraid of what they called *penelore*, or "fire canoe."

The captain wondered about the steamboat's side-wheel in another way: would it be strong enough to battle the current on their trip upstream? The earthquake had caused the river to change its course in some places and altered the shore's topography. But the Roosevelts survived the trip, as did their marriage and the *New Orleans*, proving to all that steamboats were ideal for the Ohio. Triumphantly the steamboat overtook the keelboat and flatboat in popularity.

Keelboats and flatboats transported mostly goods, not people. Steamboats provided a much more suitable means for people to travel to Cincinnati. Now that this additional type of transportation into Cincinnati had opened up, different types of people began to move in. The rough-and-rowdy keelboat men, themselves, began to settle down and attempt to become family men. Women and families began to arrive now by road and by steamboat. Keelboats were still used into the nineteenth century, but by then their day in the sun had passed. But it certainly was not the last that Cincinnatians would see of the Roosevelt family!

Starting in the mid-1800s, many changes were being made to Cincinnati's infrastructure. With increasing population after the Civil War, houses and businesses were being built but the sewer system was not keeping up with the growth. By 1870, only 671 houses were connected to city sewers. Others discharged their waste directly into the Mill Creek or Miami & Erie Canal. Homes farther away from downtown dumped their waste into creeks that then emptied into the Ohio. The sewage problem was not quickly or easily solved. In the meantime, the canal continued to fester.

Horse-drawn streetcars had begun operating in 1859 and were the preferred mode of transportation. However, as popular as the streetcars were, Cincinnatians were finding it difficult to make the trip up the many hills. Well, more accurately, the horses were finding it difficult. The hills were too steep for the horses to pull full loads up, so "inclined planes"—inclines, for short—were constructed.

This view of the Mount Adams Incline, published between 1900 and 1910 by Detroit Publishing Co., shows Rookwood Pottery to the left.

"Up the Hill by Trolley" from a book by the same name, published by
Detroit Publishing Co.

Credit: Detroit Publishing Co., State Historical Society of Colorado, Library of Congress

The Mount Auburn Incline, opening in spring 1872, was the first
to be finished. It ran from Main Street up to Jackson Hill, with a
312-foot rise over 945 feet of track. It was followed quickly by four
more inclines: the Clifton (or Bellevue), the Fairview, the Mount
Adams, and Price's Hill. A terrible accident occurred on the Mount
Auburn Incline on October 15, 1889, when the car broke free of its
cable and raced down the incline, crashing at the bottom. Three passengers died at the scene; three died later at the hospital. The other
passenger was injured but recovered. The incline was shut down and
remodeled. Eventually, this incline outlasted all the others, finally
being shut down in 1948.

The Fairview Incline ran from 1892 to 1923. It was 634 feet long—
with 207 feet of that on a trestle—and rose 210 feet. The Fairview
was the last incline to be built, opening in 1894. The Fairview was
unique in that it was originally built for streetcars, but ended up

The Price's Hill Incline was the steepest in the city, with a rise of 350 feet over only 800 feet of track.

being used by passengers only—no horses. The other inclines (save Price's Hill) were built for passengers and ended up being converted for streetcar use. The Fairview Incline ran from McMicken Avenue to Fairview Avenue.

The second incline to open (1874), Price's Hill (now called just Price Hill), ran from what is now known as lower Price Hill on Glenway Avenue to West Eighth Street. This incline had two

Starting at the turn of the century, the inclines began to show signs of wear, so the lifts that had carried horsecars and passengers up Cincinnati's steep hills one by one began to close.

Credit: Detroit Publishing Co., State Historical Society of Colorado, Library of Congress

parallel tracks for the cars to run side by side. This incline was the steepest in the city, with a rise of 350 feet over only 800 feet of track. This incline had different cars from the others: its cars, engineered by Reese Evans Price, built by his son William, and named "Highland Mary" and "Lily of the Valley" after Price's two daughters, were enclosed. Price's Hill Incline differed in another way. Most inclines were topped off by a tavern or restaurant at the top where weary (or nervous) travelers could slake their thirst with a frosty mug of Cincinnati's best beer. However, Reese and William frowned on drinking, so they did not have such an establishment. Thus the Price's Hill Incline became known as "Buttermilk Mountain."

Clifton's Incline ran 980 feet from Elm and McMicken Streets to Ohio Avenue, with a 395-foot rise. The Clifton (also known as the Bellevue Incline) ran from 1876 to 1926. Soon thereafter cable cars made their appearance, climbing the less steep—but still imposing—Gilbert Avenue from downtown to Peeble's Corner. Other neighborhoods followed suit.

Starting at the turn of the twentieth century, the inclines began to show signs of wear, so the lifts that had carried horsecars and passengers up Cincinnati's "seven" hills one by one began to close.

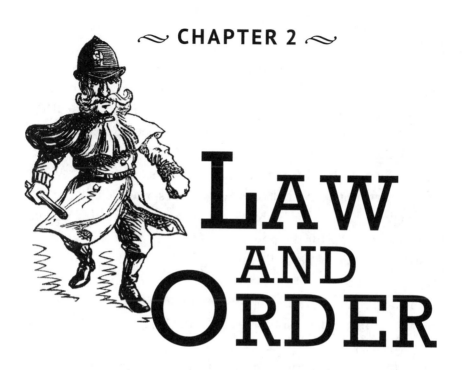

∾ CHAPTER 2 ∾

LAW
AND
ORDER

A S NEW MEANS OF TRAVEL OPENED UP, families began to trickle in and encourage other members to join them; the Burnets are a good example. Brothers David, Jacob, and George Burnet arrived in 1796 from New Jersey and were then followed by their other brother, Isaac. All four were well educated and literate and quickly became well respected as natural leaders. Unfortunately, George Burnet died in Cincinnati just a few years after his arrival. David, however, soon left for Texas, where he became the first president of the Texas Republic.

Jacob Burnet was trained as a lawyer, having studied first at Princeton and then under Judge Elisha Boudinot in Newark (Westsiders will recognize that name). According to the Ordinance of 1787, when the population reached 5,000 white male residents, a council had to be formed. So in 1799, Governor Arthur St. Clair chose 10 names and forwarded them to President John Adams. The president chose five, one of which was that of Jacob Burnet. Adams also chose Burnet to be Ohio's nonvoting representative to Congress. Burnet declined and William Henry Harrison was selected instead. As no one else on the council was a lawyer, Burnet drafted and reviewed most of the legal documents for the council.[1] The Burnets, a very large family, made an emphatic mark on the town in law, education, and politics. In 1819, Cincinnati became incorporated with Isaac Burnet as mayor.

Nicholas Longworth came to Cincinnati in 1804 at 21 to work as a law student in the office of Judge Jacob Burnet, brother of Mayor Isaac Burnet. Young "Nick" Longworth didn't stay with Judge Burnet for very long, though, as he had been bitten by the real estate bug. He had a keen eye for the potential value of land and began to buy up every little parcel he could, no matter how small and no matter who had rejected it.

The beginnings of three important families arrived in Cincinnati about this time: Judge Alphonso Taft came in 1839 from Vermont; Judge Bellamy Storer (whose son became the second husband of Maria Longworth) arrived from Maine; and Salmon P. Chase arrived from New Hampshire. These three New Englanders became the core of much of Cincinnati's identity for the next several decades.

At the end of the 1830s, after earning his law degree from Yale College, New Englander Alphonso Taft made an exploratory trip from his native Vermont out West. At the end of this trip, he settled in Cincinnati, got a job as an apprentice at a law office, and sat for the Ohio bar exam. Upon passing the bar, Taft set up his law practice.

Taft married fellow Vermonter Fanny Phelps in 1841. He became active in the First Congregational Church (Unitarian). He had been brought up a Baptist and had attended a few of Lyman Beecher's services at the Second Presbyterian Church. However, he felt the First Congregational to be most welcoming. He became a member, followed by Fanny the next year. Together they had five children, but only two survived childhood. Fanny died from tuberculosis in 1852, at which time Alphonso Taft's parents came from New England to

---

1 Fred Milligan, *Ohio's Founding Fathers* (iUniverse, 2003) p. 112.

William Howard Taft was born in this house at 60 Auburn Street in 1857. His father bought the house and two acres of land for $10,000 on June 13, 1851. It is now a National Historic Site run by the National Park Service.

Credit: Library of Congress

live with him and the two surviving boys: Charles Phelps and Peter Rawson Taft.

Taft married again the following year, this time to a Massachusetts woman named Louisa Maria ("Louise") Torrey. Together they had five more children: four boys and a girl. The first son, Samuel, died of pertussis at 14 months. The second son was William Howard Taft, who would one day become president of the United States.

Like her predecessor, Louise joined the First Congregational Church (Unitarian) after her marriage to Alphonso; she had been raised a Unitarian. Alphonso Taft often served the church as a trustee and chairman of the board. Even during his frequent travels, he stayed in close contact with the pastor and church leaders.

Politically, Taft had been a Whig, but the argument over slavery dissolved the party. In 1855 Taft became a founder of the Republican Party and participated actively in it for more than 30 years. The Republican Party was established by anti-slavery Whigs and other freethinkers who opposed slavery.

Starting in the 1840s, African Americans overtook the Irish as the second-largest ethnic group arriving in Cincinnati. Whether born free, fugitive slave or freed slave, African Americans were arriving and scooping up many jobs previously held by the Irish. Anti-black sentiments (especially from the Irish) boiled over and led to race riots in 1829, 1836, and 1841. The Fugitive Slave Law of 1850 only exacerbated the tension. In Cincinnati, the law was unevenly enforced.

One night in 1857, two escaped slaves were found in an upstairs room of a building owned by Alphonso Taft, being hidden by a Mr.

and Mrs. William Connelly. Newspaper reports at the time did not make it clear if Taft knew of the activity in his building. The Connellys were held for a short time and then let off with what amounted to a slap on the wrist.

In 1865 Alphonso Taft was appointed to the Superior Court of Cincinnati to fill a vacancy. He was subsequently elected to two more terms. Given his active role in the First Congregational Church, including his serving on the board, it is ironic, then that during his tenure as a judge he was called upon to make a decision on reading the Bible in public schools that still has ramifications today.

Since the 1820s, it had been a practice to read the Bible daily in all Cincinnati public schools: not just any Bible, but specifically the King James version. The Bible-reading was accompanied by singing Protestant hymns. Finally, in the 1860s, Archbishop John Baptist Purcell objected to the practice. When he was joined by Rabbis Isaac Mayer Wise and Max Lilienthal, the Board of Education was forced to address the matter. Two ministers sat among those on the board; both were Unitarian ministers and thus represented a very small minority of Cincinnati's religious population. One was pro-Bible-reading and the other strongly against it. The board ruled that the practice of reading the Protestant Bible in public schools should stop.

Irate, a group of Cincinnati's leading citizens immediately petitioned Cincinnati Superior Court Judge Bellamy Storer for an injunction against the Board of Education's decision. Within weeks, a trial began before the three-judge panel: Bellamy Storer, M. B. Hagans, and Alphonso Taft. The court vacated the board's decision, thus allowing Bible-reading to continue.

In his dissenting opinion, Taft wrote: "The idea that a man has less conscience because he is a rationalist, or a spiritualist, or even an atheist, than the believer in any one of the accepted forms of faith, may be current, but it is not a constitutional idea in the state of Ohio." The case was appealed to Ohio's Supreme Court where the lower court's ruling was overturned, agreeing with Taft. Unfortunately, it was a pyrrhic victory for Taft, for he was never again favored by the

Republican Party with any other appointments. Those honors were saved for another day and another Taft.

By 1873, Judge Alphonso Taft was through with his service to Ohio's Superior Court. He established a law firm—A. Taft and Sons, Attorneys at Law—and was joined by Charles Phelps and Peter Rawson Taft, his oldest two sons with Fanny Phelps. Eventually all of his sons became attorneys and practiced law except for Horace, who founded the Taft School for Boys in Watertown, Connecticut.

One favorite story told by Nick Longworth and his contemporaries was about his defending an alleged horse stealer. After Longworth got the man acquitted, the man was allowed to keep the horse he was accused of stealing. Immensely grateful, the former-alleged horse thief offered Longworth one or two (the story varied) of his moonshine stills as payment. However, when Longworth went to collect, the stills were not proffered; some "worthless" acreage along Western Row in downtown

Charles Phelps Taft made quite a mark on Cincinnati, both in the publishing world and in the arts, along with his wife, Anna "Annie" Sinton Taft.

Credit: Bain News Service, between 1910 and 1915, Library of Congress

Cincinnati was offered instead. Longworth snatched the property up.

By 1859, the land was worth $750,000; its value soon shot into the millions. Longworth became enamored with the arts of grape growing and winemaking and found much of his new land perfect for these pursuits. Nicholas Longworth, at this point, had more money, owned more land, and produced more wine than anyone else in the country.

Although he was a man of small stature (barely topping 5 feet), Longworth was big in charitable deeds. For example, he brought in workers from Switzerland and Germany and constructed housing for them. He routinely had his kitchen staff bake bread for the hungry and made it known that free bread was available at his door if people just asked for it.

As good as Longworth's judgment of potential property was, his eye for flora and fauna was even better. Maryland botanist John Adlum, who gave Longworth his first grape vines, claimed that if Longworth were thrown into the Ohio River, he would bob to the surface clutching a rare species of fish in one hand and a freshwater pearl in the other.[2]

But for all of Longworth's appreciation for land and nature, he most appreciated the fruits of the vine, specifically grapes. Longworth developed an interest in the native Catawba grape after a friend gave him a vine sample, so he reinvented himself as a vintner. At his vineyards' peak, his vines covered more than 3,000 acres, producing almost 575,000 gallons of sparkling wine.

Poet Henry Wadsworth Longfellow was a fan, and wrote an homage to the wine, the vine, and the vintner, closing with

> *While pure as a spring*
> *Is the wine I sing,*
> *And to praise it, one needs but name it;*
> *For Catawba wine*
> *Has need of no sign,*
> *No tavern-bush to proclaim it.*
>
> *And this Song of the Vine,*
> *This greeting of mine,*
> *The winds and the birds shall deliver*
> *To the Queen of the West,*
> *In her garlands dressed,*
> *On the banks of the Beautiful River.*

---

2 Iola Silberstein, *Cincinnati Then and Now* (Cincinnati: The League of Women Voters, 1982). 47.

We of the twenty-first century know that Nicholas Longworth's life's work went far beyond his vines. The Astronomical Society approached him for a monetary donation for the construction of an observatory. Instead, he surprised them by donating 4 acres of land on top of what was then known as Mount Ida.

Former president John Quincy Adams spread the first layer of mortar and laid the cornerstone on November 9, 1843, declaring the occasion a tribute to the citizens of Cincinnati and an example to the rest of the nation. The 76-year-old Adams braved failing health to make the trip because of his commitment to science and his dedication to the idea of a national observatory. (The event was Adams's last public speech before his death in 1848.) When the Cincinnati Observatory was completed in June 1845, it was the first in the nation. Mount Ida was renamed Mount Adams after the former president who had felt it was so important to make the trip to Cincinnati.

Nicholas Longworth owned two main estates, both in Cincinnati: Mayor Baum's former mansion on Pike Street downtown, and a large property bordering Grandin Road, where his neighbors were the Burnets, Grandins, Groesbecks, and Harrisons—among other Cincinnati elites. Longworth had named the Grandin estate "Rookwood" for the many crows on the property. Toward the end of Nicholas Longworth's life, he moved to Rookwood and spent the last of his days there. Nicholas Longworth died on February 10, 1863, at the age of 80.

His legacy was multifold. His beloved vineyards, unfortunately, died off from blight, but were then donated by his son, Joseph, to the city of Cincinnati to become the foundation of Eden Park. Joseph once noted that he felt people would only remember him as the son of his father (the first Nicholas) and the father of his son (Nicholas II). To some extent this is true, but his largesse is not forgotten. Besides the gift of Eden Park, he generously supported the Art Academy of Cincinnati and his own daughter, Maria (pronounced ma-RYE-ah), in her philanthropy and entrepreneurship.

Alice Roosevelt Longworth was quite a character. She had a song named after her, was related by birth and marriage to two politicians, and bore the child of a third. She knew every president from Benjamin Harrison to Jimmy Carter personally and was referred to as "the other Washington Monument."

Credit: Library of Congress

Longworth is also known for something else: his great-grandson (Nicholas Longworth III) married Alice Roosevelt, daughter of President Theodore Roosevelt. This Nicholas Longworth then went on to become a two-term speaker of the U.S. House of Representatives. Today the Longworth name is represented in Longworth Hall in the West End, and there is usually a tavern called

Mrs. William Howard (Nellie) Taft and Mrs. Nicholas (Alice) Longworth III stop to chat in their snazzy automobile. William Howard Taft's presidency is referred to as the "First Motoring Presidency" because of his passion for the new mode of transportation.

Credit: Harris & Ewing, Inc. Collection, 1955, Library of Congress

Longworth's in Mount Adams. The Longworth mansion on Fourth Street is now the site of the Taft Museum of Art.

Nicholas Longworth III, great-grandson of Nicholas Longworth I, was elected to the Ohio State Senate at the dawn of the twentieth century. The eponymous Longworth Act, which he wrote to regulate the issuance of municipal bonds, was called one of the most successful laws in Ohio's history.

Longworth was subsequently elected to the U.S. House of Representatives from Ohio's First District. In Washington, he cut a dashing figure; he was often seen carrying a gold-knobbed cane and wearing spats. A bachelor, his name was often linked with some of Washington society's most eligible debutantes. Alice Roosevelt, daughter of fellow Republican President Theodore Roosevelt, caught

Longworth's eye. They married at the White House on February 17, 1906. Longworth was 37, and Roosevelt was 22.

Meanwhile, Nick Longworth's sister, Clara Eleanor Longworth, had fallen in love with a French nobleman, the Viconte de Chambrun of France, a direct descendant of the Marquis de Lafayette. Aldeberte and Clara were married on February 19, 1901, in Cincinnati, making Clara the Comtesse de Chambrun.

By 1896 Maria Longworth Nichols Storer (aunt to Nicholas Longworth III) and her husband had become Roman Catholic. They pressed their friend Teddy Roosevelt to use his influence to help another friend, Archbishop John Ireland, to become a cardinal. This pressure did not relent as Roosevelt rose up the ranks through New York governor to president of the United States. At the same time, Maria Storer pressured Roosevelt to make her husband an ambassador to England or France. The best that Roosevelt could do in that arena was to appoint Bellamy Storer the Ambassador to Austria-Hungary, as France and England already had ambassadors who were in good health and doing satisfactory jobs.

Still the pressure from Maria Storer to make Bellamy a cardinal continued. It became clear to Roosevelt that as president of a mostly Protestant country, it was inappropriate for him to be trying to exert any influence in the naming of a cardinal. He asked Bellamy Storer to control his wife, going so far as to request, "For God's sake, tell your wife to shut up!" Finally Roosevelt had had enough of both Storers. In 1905 he removed Storer from his post. There was some unpleasant tit-for-tat in the newspapers between Mrs. Storer and President Roosevelt, but after that things quieted down. Bellamy Storer died in 1922, after which Maria Storer sold the Grandin Road property. The "twin" house was destroyed by the new owners.

Obviously, the Longworth-Roosevelt clan was not one big happy family. The Progressive Republicans were breaking away from the old conservatives in the party. Teddy Roosevelt led the Progressives; Longworth backed the conservatives, as did his fellow Cincinnatian

William Howard Taft. Alice Roosevelt Longworth sided with her father, even appearing at a speech of Nicholas Longworth's Progressive opponent. The Republication Convention of 1912 erupted into a chaotic mess with the Progressives departing to establish a third party. Longworth lost his seat, but regained it in 1914.

The Taft family continued to lead the way in Ohio and in national politics. William Howard Taft's oldest son, Robert A. Taft, desperately wanted to follow in his father's footsteps. He had graduated first in his classes at Yale and Harvard Law, and was at the top of those passing the Ohio bar back in 1913. He established the Cincinnati law firm Taft, Stettinius & Hollister, which is still a powerhouse today.

Perhaps most meaningful to Cincinnatians, Robert A. Taft wrote the groundbreaking—and air-clearing—charter for the city of Cincinnati in 1924. Prior to that, Cincinnati had been under the dark rule of George "Boss" Cox and his cronies, starting when Cox was elected to city council in 1889 at the age of 26. As with other cities' political bosses, Cox ruled the city through a web of cronies and coercion.

One strong voice crying out against Cox and his gang had been *The Cincinnati Post*, founded by Edward Willis Scripps. Finally the Cox machine broke, thanks to a stirring speech made by Murray Seasongood to the Cincinnatus Association on October 9, 1923. The Cincinnatus Association was a group of about 50 young businessmen organized by Captain Victor Heinz to address municipal problems in Cincinnati.

By this time, Cox was dead, but the machine was plowing forward under the direction of his protégé, Rudolph Hynicka. Seasongood had had enough. "We have the fourth-largest per capita expenditure of any city in the country," he told the association. "What do we get for it? Nothing, absolutely nothing. . . . I for one believe that the time has come to cut out every extra tax levy, bond issue or anything else that will give the bunch a chance to squander money. Make them produce the goods on what they have or get out."

Seasongood and Taft, with others, redrafted the city charter to call for a nine-member council to replace the 32-seat board then in place, a council-appointed city manager as chief administrator, a mayor selected by his or her council colleagues, and a proportional representation ballot. (This charter form of government took effect in 1925 and stayed in effect until it was replaced by the "strong mayor" form in 2001.)

Although Robert A. Taft held many public offices in both Ohio and Washington, he was never able to reach the Oval Office. He was, however, the first son of a president since John Quincy Adams to serve in Congress. Taft was well liked on both sides of the aisle, but could not gain a groundswell of support among Republicans. In August 1941, he voted against extending the draft. Then on December 6, 1941, he was heard questioning why an armed force of 2 million men was necessary. The next morning proved why it was necessary.

Robert Taft became President Dwight Eisenhower's trusted confidant in Congress in the 1950s, but this relationship was cut short by Taft's failing health. Four months after experiencing pain while golfing with the president, Taft died from advanced, inoperable cancer in July 1953. He was only 63 years old.

His son, Robert Taft Jr., followed in his father's political footsteps, serving four terms as a state senator and three in Washington. He, too, was ultimately defeated and chose to return to the family law firm.

Robert A. Taft III then entered the family business of holding public office, serving as a state legislator, Hamilton County commissioner, Ohio secretary of state, and finally governor. He is the fifth generation of Tafts to hold political office. His daughter, Anna, eschewed public office and instead has dedicated herself to public service of another sort. In 2006 she created the nonprofit Tandana Foundation, a cross-cultural volunteer program, to provide scholarships and funding for small community projects and health care volunteer mission trips in highland Ecuador and Mali's Dogon Country, located in sub-Saharan Africa. ("Tandana" means "to gather together" or "to unite" in Kichwa, an indigenous language of the Andes.) Both Bob Taft and former Ohio first lady Hope Taft are very supportive of their daughter's work and in carrying out its missions.

Meanwhile, Charles Phelps Taft's kin have not been slackers, either. His son, Charles Phelps Taft II, helped create a new city charter and form of government in Cincinnati to break the Republican hold on the city. He was elected to the position of Hamilton County prosecutor in 1926, followed by a city council seat in 1937. During World War II, "Charlie" Taft served in the Roosevelt Administration in several capacities, earning him the moniker "New Deal Republican." He remained in the Cincinnati city hall until he retired at age 80 in 1977. He died at age 85 in June 1983 and is buried in Spring Grove Cemetery in the Taft family plot.

William Howard Taft said that sitting on the Supreme Court was his life's most meaningful accomplishment. He did not enjoy being president, and—having battled a weight problem since childhood—when he was unhappy, he ate. That is probably why he is known best nationally as the president who once got stuck in a bathtub and had a bathtub large enough for four grown men in the White House. Although no definitive proof exists of Taft's bathtub predicament, in his book, *42 Years in the White House*, Ike Hoover noted that the unfortunate incident had occurred. As Hoover had been chief White House usher during Taft's presidency, this probably confirms it. William Howard Taft served on the Supreme Court until just a month before his death in March 1930.

President Taft's friend Nicholas Longworth was finding political success but not personal success. After Alice Roosevelt Longworth's political disloyalty, the marriage faltered. Rumors surrounded the couple concerning mutual infidelity. Before their marriage, Alice—an independent, strong-minded young woman—had no shortage of courtiers. This did not stop during her marriage, despite the 1925 birth of their only child, Paulina Longworth. In her diary, Alice Longworth admitted that Paulina was the result of a long-term affair with Senator William Borah from Idaho. Despite this, Nicholas Longworth adored Paulina and she returned his affection. Paulina

When someone sent William Howard Taft this photo, he wrote back, "I note your enclosure of the photograph of my three brothers and myself. There is a good deal of avoirdupois [extra weight] and length in that group. It was a family meeting in Cincinnati where we met to take part in the dedication of a new building called the Alphonso Taft Hall, for the housing of the Law School of the University of Cincinnati, and it is a great pleasure to have secured a photograph of this kind." From left to right, they are Henry Waters Taft, Chief Justice Taft, Charles Phelps Taft, and Horace Dutton Taft.

was devastated at the age of 6 when Longworth died in 1931. It was the end of the Longworth line.

Alphonso Taft died in 1891 in San Diego, California, where he had moved for health reasons. Although William is the most famous of Alphonso's children nationally, locally Charles Phelps Taft was also a very prominent citizen. He became publisher of the *Cincinnati Times-Star* (which was later bought out by the *Cincinnati Post*). He served as treasurer of the May Festival board for many years and was a staunch supporter of both the Cincinnati Zoo and the Cincinnati Symphony.

William himself had a typical Cincinnati childhood by most accounts. He attended Woodward High School, where some called him "Big Lub" (for his size) or "Howard," but mostly "Old Bill." After earning a bachelor of arts from Yale University in New Haven, Connecticut, he returned to Cincinnati where he earned a bachelor of law from UC's College of Law. He graduated and was admitted to the bar in 1880. Upon graduating, his first job was as a legal reporter for the *Cincinnati Times*.

In 1881 he became an assistant prosecutor for Hamilton County, Ohio, a position he held for two years until leaving to enter private practice. During that time he married Helen Louise ("Nellie") Herron, the daughter of Judge John Williamson Herron, a law partner of Rutherford B. Hayes. Taft ended up following his father's footsteps into the Superior Court of Cincinnati, being appointed in 1887. He resigned in 1890 after being appointed United States Solicitor-General by President Benjamin Harrison.

Mrs. William Howard (Nellie) Taft, in the meantime, was quite busy in Cincinnati. Through the efforts of many, the Cincinnati Symphony Orchestra had formed—only the fifth such orchestra in the country. Mrs. Taft, along with two other Cincinnati ladies and abetted by $15,000 in capital, organized the first series of concerts in 1895. She became president of the CSO and served in this function for many years until succeeded by Mrs. Christian (Bettie

A statue of William Howard Taft stands outside the University of Cincinnati College of Law. Passersby often wonder if the statue is life sized or not.

Credit: Andrew Higley/UC Photo Services

Fleischman) Holmes, who was then succeeded by Mrs. Charles P. (Anna Sinton) Taft.

President Warren G. Harding named fellow Ohioan and former U.S. president William Howard Taft Chief Justice of the United States in 1921. Actually, President Theodore Roosevelt had offered Taft a Supreme Court appointment multiple times previously, but Taft had refused. At the time, Taft had been civil governor of Cuba and was heavily involved in developments in the Philippines.

But when the chief justice position was left vacant by the death of Edward Douglass White, Taft eagerly accepted the offer. Ironically, by accepting the Supreme Court appointment, he replaced a man whom he had appointed. (He was also succeeded as chief justice by another of his appointments.) As chief justice of the United States, William Howard Taft administered the oath of office to presidents Calvin Coolidge and Woodrow Wilson. He was the only former president to ever do so.

In 1925 the University of Cincinnati dedicated its new College of Law building. In attendance were four of the Taft brothers, from eldest to youngest Charles Phelps Taft, William Howard Taft, Henry Waters Taft, and Horace Dutton Taft. When someone sent him a photograph of the event, he responded with a letter in which he wrote, "I note your enclosure of the photograph of my three brothers and myself. There is a good deal of avoirdupois [extra weight] and length in that group. It was a family meeting in Cincinnati where we met to take part in the dedication of a new building called the Alphonso Taft Hall, for the housing of the Law School of the University of Cincinnati, and it is a great pleasure to have secured a photograph of this kind."

At the time, Henry was a lawyer, Charles was publisher of the *Cincinnati Times-Star*, and Horace was headmaster of the Taft School for Boys in Connecticut. William, of course, was a former president and the chief justice of the United States. The Tafts were surely a family that had a way with words.

Hail to the Chiefs

Ohio wrestles with Massachusetts and Virginia for the title of "state to produce the most presidents." Both Ohio and Virginia proclaim themselves the "Mother of Presidents" with eight each. Unfortunately, both lay claim to William Henry Harrison. Although Harrison was born in Virginia and didn't move to Cincinnati until he was a teenager, he claimed Ohio as his home. (Incidentally, he was also governor of the Indiana Territory from 1800 to 1812, so they might want him, too. But they're not in the running for the "Mother of Presidents" title, so they can claim him all they want.) As for Massachusetts, it depends on whether George Herbert Walker Bush identifies himself as a Yankee or a Texan.

In case you're wondering, Virginia's eight are George Washington, Thomas Jefferson, James Madison, James Monroe, William Henry Harrison, John Tyler, Zachary Taylor, and Woodrow Wilson. Ohio's eight are William Henry Harrison, Ulysses S. Grant, Rutherford B. Hayes, James Garfield, Benjamin Harrison, William McKinley, William Howard Taft, and Warren G. Harding.

Not only do many presidents come from Ohio, but a number of them also had roots in the Queen City, starting with one teenager who arrived from Virginia by way of the University of Pennsylvania. William Henry Harrison had been studying medicine, but was forced to leave when his father died. As the youngest son in a large family, he knew he was not going to get much of his father's estate. He joined the army as an ensign (the lowest officer's rank) in the 16th U.S. Infantry. He arrived in Cincinnati in November 1791 to a cold-shouldered welcome. The rest of the officers at Fort Washington had been supporting one of their own to get the position, but Harrison quickly won them over.

Harrison was soon promoted to lieutenant and in 1793 became an aide-de-camp to General "Mad Anthony" Wayne. General Wayne felt Harrison's service as an aide—including providing occasional medical care—was invaluable during the Battle of Fallen Timbers. In 1794 Harrison was promoted to captain. When General Wayne died, Captain Harrison became commander of Fort Washington.

One person young Harrison did not impress, however, was John Cleves Symmes. In fact, when Harrison asked Symmes for his daughter Anna's hand in marriage, Symmes refused. So William and Anna waited until Symmes was traveling to the other side of the Northwest Territory and then eloped. Of Harrison, Symmes once said, "He can neither bleed, plead, nor preach, and if he could plow I should be satisfied."

On March 4, 1841, William Henry Harrison was inaugurated as the ninth president of the United States. It was a foul day, with biting winds and low temperatures. The soon-to-be president was urged to bundle up against the snow. Still seeing himself as the indefatigable, unconquerable soldier of his youth, he refused all source of warmth and delivered a 90-minute inaugural address of 8,445 words. He developed a respiratory infection and died one month later to the day.

To this date, William Henry Harrison holds the records for the shortest U.S. presidency *and* the longest inaugural speech. One can't help but wonder if a shorter speech might have meant a longer presidency. Ohioans must be a chatty bunch. William Henry Harrison's inaugural speech was the longest, with William Howard Taft's and Benjamin Harrison's running a distant second (5,433 words) and fourth (4,388 words) respectively.

Ohio has not had someone in the Oval Office since Warren G. Harding, who died suddenly while on a trip. (Some speculated that he had been poisoned by his wife.) Of the eight presidents who have died in office, four of them were from Ohio: two by assassination, two by natural causes.

～ CHAPTER 3 ～

GOING PLACES

For a while early in the new century, it looked as if more settlers and visitors would be rushing to Ohio by a new means: paved road. On March 29, 1806, Thomas Jefferson signed the Maryland Act to begin laying the paved Cumberland Road from Maryland to Ohio. The road was to be constructed using varied stone sizes in a new process named macadam for the Scottish engineer who invented it, J. S. MacAdam.

Construction on what became known as the National Road began in 1811 at Cumberland. The National Road reached Ohio's eastern border at Wheeling, West Virginia, in 1818. However, a debate began that stopped construction for several years over whether the federal government had the authority to build a road. When construction finally started up again, the road never got any closer to Cincinnati than Springfield, Ohio, about 80 miles to the northeast.

Between a Rock and a Hard Place

The Ohio River was much shallower before the U.S. Army Corps of Engineers deepened the channel. Although in 1824 the Corps had been given charge to clear the river of snags, sandbars, and debris, the natural river depth still varied over the course of a year. Although the natural depth of the Ohio near Cincinnati was between 3 and 20 feet, at times during the year the depth was barely 12 inches. Other times, like during the spring thaws and rainy season, the river could swell to great depths, such as 80 feet deep, 28 feet above flood stage (as in 1937) or 71 feet deep (as in 1884).

Modern readers of Harriet Beecher Stowe's *Uncle Tom's Cabin* and Toni Morrison's *Beloved* might have wondered how fleeing slaves could cross such a deep, swift river as the Ohio. Well, it was nowhere near as deep then as it is today, but to a non-swimmer back then the Ohio was no doubt terrifying regardless of the depth.

Still many slaves braved the Ohio, deep or not, for slavery was illegal in Ohio, right from the very start. The Northwest Ordinance of 1787, which brought John Cleves Symmes and his party to Ohio in the first place, had forbidden involuntary servitude except as punishment for a crime. Nevertheless, many white southerners moved into Ohio, expecting to keep "their" slaves.

Ohioans were torn. Not surprisingly, their views often depended on where they had emigrated from before landing in Cincinnati. Starting in 1807, however, the state legislature began passing a series of "Black Laws" making it increasingly difficult for free people of color to settle in the state. Every black person was required to pay a bond of $1,500 as a guarantee of good behavior. No person of color could testify in court against a white person. Black people were prevented from entering public institutions such as schools, hospitals, the asylum, and the poorhouse.

As would be the case 100 years later during the Civil Rights movement, the African American community was also torn. Some started petitions to have the Black Laws repealed. Some fled farther north into Canada. Some stayed right here to fight for their homes. As Alvin Harlow put it in his 1950 book, *The Serene Cincinnatians:*

"Nowhere else in our history has there been a city situated quite as was Cincinnati in those years; a city on free soil, yet just across a narrow river from slavery and deriving most of its essential trade from that area; a city where idealism, humanitarianism, and the New England conscience were forced into a bitter battle with self-interest; a city where Northern blood predominated in the greater concerns of business and industry, but whose very life seemed to depend upon maintenance of friendship with the slave-holding South by tacit condonation of its chief sin."

Cincinnati occupied a strange position as the Civil War approached—politically, geographically, and emotionally. It did business with both the North and the South. Cincinnati's large German population tended to support the fledgling Republican Party, while the city's largest newspaper—*The Cincinnati Daily Enquirer*—supported the South and the Democrats. Despite its now-famous stations on the Underground Railroad and strong abolitionist voices such as those of Salmon P. Chase, Levi Coffin, and Lyman Beecher, Cincinnati was home to just as many who supported slavery. Charles R. Wilson, in "Cincinnati's Reputation During the Civil War," said, "Cincinnati's slogan from 1861 to 1865 might well have been 'Peace—with the Constitution as it is, the Union as it was, and the negroes where they are.'"

Overall, Cincinnati seemed to just prefer the status quo. Don't rock the boat. (Or the bridge, either.)

Nevertheless, Ohio supported the war, with Ohioans fighting in every major battle—wearing the blue *and* the gray. Several Civil War generals came from Ohio, including Ulysses S. Grant (whose horse was named "Cincinnati"), Rutherford B. Hayes (who became president of the United States), William H. Lytle (who was killed in action), Ormsby M. Mitchel (who returned to Cincinnati to erect the Observatory), George A. Custer (who later died in the Battle of Little Bighorn), William T. Sherman (known for burning his way to the Atlantic), and Charles Clark (born in Cincinnati, became a Confederate general and later governor of Mississippi).

So thus is Cincinnati described: it faces the South. Kentucky was a slave-holding state; Ohio was not. Cincinnati was a mix of abolitionists, slave-owners, Underground Railroad conductors, freemen, former slaves, and slave hunters. And now it houses the National Underground Railroad Freedom Center.

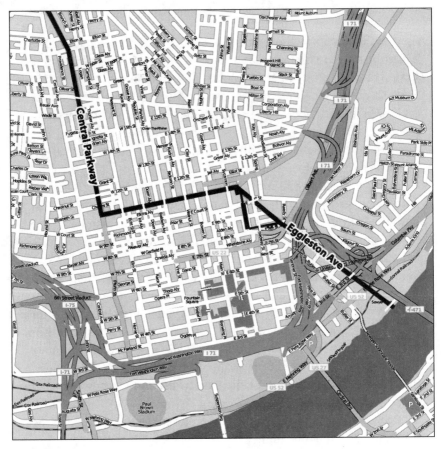

The blue line in this diagram shows the course of the old Miami & Erie Canal overlying a more modern map of Cincinnati.

Source: http://en.wikipedia.org/wiki/Miami_and_Erie_Canal

In the meantime, Ohio waited and relied on its newfound love of the steamboat. And just when it looked as if the steamboat was queen of the water, something else came around the corner and right into town: a canal.

The Miami & Erie Canal, built from 1825 to 1845 to connect Cincinnati to Lake Erie in Toledo, helped carry Cincinnati's pork products to an even larger, more eager market. Elias Kahn didn't start his meat business until 1883, but the foundations had already been laid.

The Miami & Erie Canal rounded the curve on Plum Street as it came into town.

Credit: Library of Congress

In 1822, President James Monroe had vetoed a bill to raise funds for extending the National Road by placing toll gates on it. He felt that the federal government did not have the right to levy tolls. The bill was redrafted, with the national government building the road and then turning it over to the states. With this change, Monroe felt he could approve it and did so.

July 4, 1825, was a particularly auspicious day in the Midwest. After President James Monroe's 1824 authorization of the bill for further spending on the National Road, ground was broken in Ohio for extending the road that had begun all the way back East in Maryland. Construction on the road was delayed a few more times by politics, changes in plans, and funding problems. But on that very same day in 1825, ground was also broken for the Ohio & Erie and Miami & Erie Canals.

A typical boat travels down the canal near Mohawk Street. Soon talk of
a subway would be heard but then abandoned for a beautiful paved road:
Central Parkway.

Credit: Library of Congress

Construction began on the canals in 1825 and concluded on the
Ohio & Erie Canal by 1833. Cincinnati's portion of the Miami &
Erie Canal was completed as far as Middletown by 1829, and as far
as Dayton by the 1830s. (However, it took until 1845 to finish the
entire stretch to Toledo.) By today's street names, the canal followed
Central Parkway south into town, then continued east until it ran
into what is now Eggleston. From there it followed Eggleston's path
to the Ohio River.

The canals could accommodate different kinds of boats. The
barges, which were the slow beasts of burden, were up to 78 feet long
and 14 feet wide. These boats could carry up to 60 tons of freight and
were pulled by horses or mules walking along the bank. Passengers
were transported in lighter packet boats that could seat people above
or below deck. Packet boats could carry up to 40 people and also
carried the mail.

Cincinnati's canal turned out to provide more than just a means of transportation for businesses. It also provided entertainment to youths for swimming on hot days and skating on cold ones, water for quenching fires, and ice for cooling beer at the many taverns. The canal also became known as something else. With an influx of immigrating Germans, the canal must have reminded them of the Rhine, and thus the canal became the border of the neighborhood known as Over-the-Rhine.

The canal became an immediate sensation, reducing both the time and cost of transporting Cincinnati's goods to northern markets. Cincinnati was about to become the producer of even more goods, with two marriages made in heaven, thanks to a candlemaker named Alexander Norris.

Cincinnati had enjoyed a transportation heyday in the 1840s with its proximity to the Ohio River, its canal, its roads, and its rail. However, in relying so much on its waterways, Cincinnatians had been slow to embrace railroads as a necessity. Although many north-south routes ran through Cincinnati, east-west routes tended to run north of the city. Goods from the northeastern cities of Boston, New York, and Philadelphia were on their way to Cleveland and Chicago, bypassing Cincinnati and its wares. In the 1860s, the Civil War closed the Ohio River to commercial shipping, further paralyzing Cincinnati's ability to market its goods.

Mostly abandoned by 1910, the Cincinnati stretch of the Miami & Erie Canal had been drained in 1919 into the Ohio River. Initially

The flatboats and the steamboats were still sharing the waters in the first decades of the twentieth century, but not for long.

Credit: "Waterfront of Cincinnati, O." June 1914 by A. O. Kraemer Art Co., Library of Congress

Before They Were Bridges

A distinct landmark in Cincinnati is the Ohio River, which functions as the southern border of the city and the state. That border is right at the water's edge, as the Commonwealth of Kentucky owns the Ohio River. (Well, it owns the river *bottom*.) If an Ohio resident wishes to get married on one of the riverboats, the boat must heave to the Cincinnati side during the "legal" part of the ceremony.

Many bridges connect Cincinnati to its southern neighbor. Given whose water they pass over, it should come as no surprise that of the four bridges named for people, three of them are named for Kentuckians. The fourth proudly bears the name of the builder of the Brooklyn Bridge, John A. Roebling, as a bold reminder that he built *our* suspension bridge first. What might be surprising, however, is that the Roebling Suspension Bridge, the first of the bridges, was built during the Civil War.

At the brink of the war, Cincinnati was the wealthiest Northern city that bordered the South. However, part of that wealth and much of Cincinnati's growth was because of its proximity to the South. Although part of a free state, many Cincinnatians had relatives in the South, wearing the gray and sympathizing with the rebellion.

Ohio's Governor William Dennison was advised to order "Columbiads" —large caliber, smoothbore, muzzle-loading cannons that were able to fire heavy projectiles at both high and low trajectories. These were to be mounted on Cincinnati's hills and aimed at Kentucky. To say that Cincinnatians were conflicted would be an understatement.

A contingent from Cincinnati paid a call upon Kentucky's Governor Beriah Magoffin to seek his assurance that Kentucky would do nothing that could be perceived as "menacing." Much discussion followed, both on the state and local level. Governor Dennison wanted to keep trade open between Kentucky and Ohio as long as Kentucky was not in "open rebellion." The nervous people in Cincinnati, however, didn't feel that was good enough. They sought Kentucky's assurance that they would be loyal to the Union or shipping would cease.

Judge Bellamy Storer spoke for the Cincinnatians: "This is no time for soft words. We feel, as you have a right to feel, that you have a governor who cannot be depended upon in this crisis. But it is on the men of Kentucky that we rely. All we want to know is whether you are for the Union, without reservation. Brethren of Kentucky! The men of the North have been your friends, and they still desire to be. But I will speak plainly. . . . There is a point which cannot be passed. While we rejoice in your friendship, while we glory in your bravery, we would have you understand that we are your equals as well as your friends."

Although Kentucky assured the Cincinnati contingent that they wanted no part in the rebellion, they were pleased with Governor Dennison's view. The Cincinnatians were not; they gathered four days later to pass the following: "*Resolved* that any men or set of men in Cincinnati or elsewhere, who knowingly sell or ship one ounce of flour or pound of provisions, or any arms or articles which are contraband of war, to any person or any State which has not declared its firm determination to sustain the Government in the present crisis, is a traitor, and deserves the doom of a traitor."

Despite the turmoil going on around it, the Covington & Cincinnati Suspension Bridge was opened to foot travel on December 1, 1866, perhaps a testimony to the regional relationship between Ohio and Kentucky that transcended the national rift between North and South. It leads our list of bridges, in order of appearance:

1) **1866–67, John A. Roebling Suspension Bridge (originally called the Covington & Cincinnati Suspension Bridge):** At the time the bridge was built, it was the longest suspension bridge in the world and the first to use both vertical suspenders and diagonal stays fanning from either tower. What enabled Roebling to create this wonder were some of his previous patents on wire rope, which he then found a way to spin into heavy iron wire cables right on site. He also developed a simple way to anchor these cables. All of these ideas were groundbreaking; without them, neither Cincinnati's nor the Brooklyn Bridge would exist. Roebling sustained a foot injury while working on Brooklyn, and developed tetanus. He died shortly after

the Brooklyn Bridge was begun so the work fell to his son, Washington A. Roebling. In 1984, our bridge was officially renamed the John A. Roebling Suspension Bridge, but most Cincinnatians just call it "the Suspension Bridge."

2) **1872, Newport & Cincinnati RR Bridge:** This bridge, originally just a single standard gauge railroad track, was bought by the Louisville & Nashville Railroad in 1904 and renamed the L&N Bridge. At the same time the cart and horse dirt path that had been added in the 1890s was paved for automobile traffic. In the 1950s, the L&N Bridge was made one way during rush hour to enhance traffic in and out of Cincinnati at peak load times. The bridge was closed to railroad traffic in 1987. It fell into disrepair and was finally closed to automobile traffic in 2003. It was painted purple and reopened in its new life as a pedestrian-only bridge, nicknamed the "Purple People Bridge," in 2004. For a while, climbing tours were offered on top of its arches.

3) **1877, Cincinnati Southern RR Bridge:** Connecting Cincinnati and Ludlow, Kentucky, this bridge was built for the city-owned Cincinnati Southern Railroad. The bridge was refurbished in 1922 and now is used by the Norfolk Southern Railway. It is the busiest railroad bridge in the city.

4) **1889, Chesapeake & Ohio RR Bridge:** This bridge connects Cincinnati and Covington. It was refurbished in 1929. Its piers were extended and are used by the Clay Wade Bailey Bridge.

5) **1890, Cincinnati & Newport Bridge, (a.k.a. the "Central Bridge"):** This bridge, built between the L&N and Roebling bridges, was the first standard cantilever truss bridge ever built. The deck of the Central Bridge was composed of metal grating that made for a noisy, rough ride over its length. The northern approach to the bridge did not line up directly with Broadway, so an "S"-curve was inserted. It was destroyed in 1992 and replaced by the Taylor-Southgate Bridge, still with an S-curve on the northern approach.

The Covington & Cincinnati Suspension Bridge was opened to foot traffic on December 1, 1866, a testimony to the strong relationship between Cincinnati and Northern Kentucky that transcended the national rift between North and South.

Credit: Library of Congress

the bed of the canal was to be used for a subway in Cincinnati. However, with the growing popularity of the automobile, interest in a rail system had waned. The plan was scotched in 1927 in favor of filling in the canal, and in 1928 Central Parkway was dedicated.

Steamboats provided both entertainment and transportation. They also faced their share of trouble. The first *Island Queen*, a popular excursion boat ridden by visitors to Old Coney, caught fire in a conflagration at Cincinnati's public landing and burned to the waterline in 1922. The *Morning Star, Island Maid, Chris Greene*, and *Tacoma* were completely destroyed in the same fire.

6) **1963, Brent Spence Bridge:** Named for Kentuckian Brent Spence, this bridge carries I-71 and I-75 from Cincinnati to Covington. Spence, who graduated from the University of Cincinnati with a law degree, was elected to the U.S. House of Representatives, where he served from 1931 to 1963. He died in 1967 at the age of 92. The Brent Spence Bridge is a cantilever truss bridge with two decks: southbound on top and northbound on the bottom. It is one of the most heavily traveled bridges in the nation and is under consideration for renovation or replacement.

7) **1974, Clay Wade Bailey Bridge:** This cantilever bridge carries automobile traffic on U.S. Routes 42 and 127 from Cincinnati to Covington. Clay Wade Bailey was a well-respected Kentucky journalist, born in 1905. He suffered a stroke in 1973 and died the following year.

8) **1977, Daniel Carter Beard Bridge:** Daniel Carter Beard was an artist and nature lover who created the illustrations for the original version of Mark Twain's *A Connecticut Yankee in King Arthur's Court.* He turned his love of the outdoors and exploring into a group he called "Sons of Daniel Boone," which eventually became the Boy Scouts of America. The Daniel Carter Beard Bridge carries I-471 from Cincinnati to Newport, Kentucky. Because of its bright yellow arches, it is often referred to as the "Big Mac."

9) **1995, Taylor-Southgate Bridge:** This continuous-truss bridge connects Newport, Kentucky, with Pete Rose Way in Cincinnati. The pedestrian walkway on the north end, in fact, leads right up to the plaza of U.S. Bank Arena. This bridge has been criticized for being rather plain for a modern bridge in a large city. It is a quiet gem, however, with very few people having discovered it.

The bottom line for Cincinnatians is that they can get to Kentucky in many ways! Our bridges also make it challenging for tugboat captains to guide their barges up and down the river with their loads of coal. One captain once said that as soon as they were through one bridge, they had to immediately line up for the next bridge in order to make it through safely. If the bridges get too busy, there's always the Anderson Ferry!

～ CHAPTER 4 ～

RAISING OUR SPIRITS

IN AUGUST 1810, near the Ohio River at the base of Race Street, something happened that surely gave the Night Watchmen lots of business: David Embree opened the first Cincinnati brewery. At its peak (or its nadir, depending on your opinion of Carrie Nation's hatchet) a hundred years later, Cincinnati had more than 30 breweries supplying about 300 saloons. Cincinnati was the leader in beer production this side of Europe.

Right about this time, a young man was making his way from Bavaria to Cincinnati. His first few jobs earned him mere pennies a day, half of which he had to spend on room and board. Finally his hard work paid off, and he began to accumulate some savings.

In 1842, at the age of 24, Christian Moerlein was able to open his own blacksmithing business. He married Sophia Adams from Strasburg the following year and had three children with her. Sadly, he lost Sophia and two of their children in the cholera epidemics. Only his son John survived. Moerlein remarried in 1849, this time to a fellow Bavarian, Barbara Oeh, who gave him nine more children, of whom seven survived.

In 1853 Moerlein sold his blacksmithing business and, with a little help from his friends, constructed a brewery on the same site. Less than a year later, he sold his first beer. Within 12 years, he had bought out his partner for $130,000. When Moerlein died in 1897, his assets exceeded $1.5 million—quite an achievement for a man who had arrived in Cincinnati penniless and barely able to speak English. His fellow beer baron Gottlieb Mühlhauser and John Hauck also became millionaires.

Unlike the breweries, which were just beginning to get started in the middle of the nineteenth century, the Ohio wine industry hit its peak in 1859 with 568,000 gallons of wine produced, most of it Catawba. Rumors of even better land for the Catawba grape farther north in Ohio never bore fruit. Powder mildew and black rot were hitting many vineyards hard, wiping out entire crops. Nicholas Longworth spent his final days looking for another grape that might better withstand the rot. His dying words were for his vintner son-in-law, W. J. Flagg. Just before slipping into unconsciousness, he asked if Flagg had arrived. He said he wanted to tell him of a new vine he had found that was resistant to mildew and rot.

Another fine-spirited Cincinnatian of the late 1880s was John Goetz Jr. He had married Elisabeth Moerlein, making him Christian Moerlein's son-in-law. A lawyer by trade, he was the vice president of his father-in-law's Christian Moerlein Brewing Company. He was also very active in the community, sitting on several boards, such as the Cincinnati Board of Fire Commissioners, and serving as the president of the Cincinnati Zoo. He was well liked nationally as well as locally.

Goetz died suddenly in 1899 from a stroke, just five days short of his 44th birthday (and only two years after Moerlein himself). On his passing, the *American Brewers' Review* (Volume 12) said:

"John Goetz was essentially a man of the people. Of humble origin he won his spurs on the battlefield of life by dint of high courage, honesty of purpose and noble energy. . . . Mr. Goetz was one of the moving spirits in organizing the Brewers' exchange. . . . John Goetz did a great deal to advance the interests of the brewers, and along lines which elevated the business. . . . He was known to brewers all over the United States as a progressive able man. . . . The Jubilee Saengerfest planned for next June lost in him one of its stanchest [sic] supporters. . . . In fact he was active in almost every movement that tended to promote the interests or improve the conditions of the citizens of Cincinnati."

Despite the deaths of both Moerlein and Goetz, Cincinnati was certainly not at a loss for beer. The Christian Moerlein Brewing Company was still in the capable hands of Christian's son, William. (The Goetz house was bought in the 1960s by the Lenhardt family and for many years was the home of Lenhardt's German-Hungarian restaurant and Christie's *bier-*  *garten* in the Clifton Heights area of Cincinnati. Sadly, after half a century of serving fine schnitzel and spaetzle, Lenhardt's and Christie's closed in 2013 and the building was razed.)

Louis Hudepohl and George Kotte owned a wholesale liquor business. When Hudepohl Sr. died, his son, Louis Hudepohl II, and Kotte bought the Koehler Brewery (formerly the Buckeye Brewery). Louis II began to buy out his partner. When Kotte died at the age of 56, Hudepohl finalized buying out Kotte's widow, Katharina, but retained the name of the brewery. He changed the name to Hudepohl Brewery when Katharina died six years later.

The United States was moving toward Prohibition, but the Eighteenth Amendment had not been ratified yet. Still, animosity was growing toward those who brewed and consumed

Ich bin von Zinzinnati

A storm was brewing in Europe with repercussions as far away as the Ohio Valley. Many German-Americans in Cincinnati, and elsewhere, wanted to keep the United States out of the war in Europe. Before the war, Judge Alfred K. Nippert had served as the vice president of the American Commission for Relief of East Prussia. The funds raised in Cincinnati alone had helped rebuild one Prussian (German) village. On June 24, 1916, a delegation from the commission, including Judge Nippert, visited Kaiser Wilhelm II. Upon his return to the United States, Nippert conveyed the Kaiser's message of peace to President Woodrow Wilson.

As alliances were forged and broken in Europe leading up to and during World War I, tensions began building in Cincinnati as well. Strong anti-German emotions swelled, affecting both families and landmarks. (Besides becoming anti-German, Cincinnati was also becoming vocally anti-beer and anti-Catholic, too.)

When the United States entered World War I, Americans began to look at all things German with suspicion—including German-Americans. The public library was asked to remove all German books from its shelves. German streets were renamed, often just by turning them backward. Some people with German names Americanized them, changing "Wilhelm" to "William" or "Zimmerman" to "Carpenter," for example. In some cases, names were changed for families when coming through Ellis Island by clerks who didn't recognize or couldn't spell the unfamiliar names. So "Müller" might have been written as "Miller" and left that way by a family wanting to assimilate.

In 1918, federal marshal Michael Devanney ordered many locations in Cincinnati to be off-limits to Germans, including Burnet Woods, the Carthage Fair, and the Medical College building. Anyone who wanted to enter the fairground had to have a permit signed by Devanney.

alcohol, including beer. The breweries were predominantly owned by Germans.

Prohibition—the era during which the manufacture, sale, and transportation of intoxicating liquors was outlawed by ratification of the Eighteenth Amendment to the Constitution—began in 1920. For the next 13 years, Cincinnati was affected as was the rest of the nation by this amendment and by the Volstead Act. However, in a way, Cincinnati's loss was worse: by the 1880s, Cincinnati had become the mecca of beer-brewing. Virtually all, if not all, of the 20 to 30 breweries were owned by German-American or German families. Many Cincinnatians felt that Prohibition took on an anti-German focus. As the axe of Prohibition fell, the last of Cincinnati's breweries to remain were the John Hauck Brewing Company, the Windisch-Mühlhauser Lion Brewery, and Christian Moerlein.

~ CHAPTER 5 ~

To Your Health

I N 1788, AT ABOUT THE SAME TIME that Columbia and Losantiville were settled, the Drake family came down the Ohio River from the Pittsburgh area to settle in Limestone, Kentucky. Little did the Drakes realize it, but five years later another family arrived that would change the Drake family forever. General Jared Mansfield's son Edward—only 4 at the time of his Cincinnati "debut"—became Daniel Drake's friend, co-author, biographer, and brother-in-law. In his time, Edward Mansfield became the youngest graduate in the history of West Point, attended Princeton, and eventually earned a degree in law. He practiced law for a short time in Cincinnati with Ormsby Macknight Mitchel as his partner, but he ultimately preferred journalism to the other careers for which he had been trained.

Twenty-two-year-old William Goforth, a member in the Drake party, had been studying medicine in New York. Because many medical schools had been closed during the Revolutionary War, men interested in becoming doctors studied under other doctors but couldn't obtain actual medical degrees. "Doctor" Goforth was one such man.

Goforth and the Drake family—including the oldest son, Daniel, born in 1785—lived in Limestone throughout most of Daniel's childhood. He attended a one-room schoolhouse, studying under a teacher whose knowledge barely surpassed Daniel's own. Daniel's formal schooling stopped by the time he was 9. [1]

Goforth was tapped to replace Cincinnati's Dr. Richard Allison, so Goforth left Limestone in the spring of 1800. Isaac Drake and Daniel followed him to Cincinnati in December. Isaac Drake arranged with Goforth to take then-15-year-old Daniel on as an apprentice. For $400, Goforth agreed to keep Daniel in his own home for four years and teach him the healing arts of medicine, midwifery, and curing disease, so that Daniel could become a doctor in his own right.

How ironic that Daniel Drake—known for his letters, intelligence, and literary and medical accomplishments—received his schooling from a man who could teach Daniel little more than the rule of threes in math and received his medical training from a man who wasn't really a doctor. Dr. John Stites entered Goforth's practice, so Daniel was able to finally get genuine medical training. As Stites had acquired a medical degree in Philadelphia, Daniel was able to advance his medical knowledge. Finally he had saved enough money to formally pursue a medical education.

In 1805, 20-year-old Daniel Drake prepared to return to the East coast to attend the University of Pennsylvania to obtain a legal medical degree. As he was about to depart, his beloved mentor William Goforth presented him with what writer Edward Mansfield (and Drake's future brother-in-law) described as an "autograph diploma." The document attested to Drakes studies under Goforth, who signed it as "Surgeon-General of the First Division of Ohio Militia."

Mansfield noted that it was most likely "the first medical diploma ever granted in the interior valley of North America." [2]

Despite great financial hardship, often requiring Drake to borrow books from fellow medical students, he persevered. His money ran out before he could finish the degree. Drake returned to the West in the spring of 1806. He didn't immediately return to Cincinnati, but rather spent some time visiting his family. When he did move back to Cincinnati, he brought his much younger brother, Benjamin, with him. So in 1807, Daniel and Benjamin Drake moved to Cincinnati. (In the winter of 1815–16, Drake returned to Philadelphia to finish his medical degree for good. He was the first Ohio doctor to do so.)

Drake's presence in Cincinnati affected the city in many ways. Drake's influence in the Cincinnati medical community is well known. For starters, he was one of the first doctors in Cincinnati who actually had a medical degree. His efforts most famously resulted in the establishment of the Commercial Hospital, which eventually included a building for the treatment of those with infectious diseases, an asylum, and an orphanage.

Cincinnati's children did not have consistent opportunities for schooling in the early 19th century. Attempts headed up by religious groups never quite took root, until one "Lancastrian" school was backed by a variety of denominations with Judge Jacob Burnet as president.

The "Lancaster" method called upon older students to assist with teaching and monitoring the younger students (thus not requiring as many paid teachers). The school also had the support of multiple churches in Cincinnati and was therefore more universally supported among its citizens, yet membership in a particular church—or any church—was not a criterion to be on the board of directors. Many Methodists provided financial backing; the Presbyterians provided the land.

---

2 Mansfield, p. 66

This "Lancaster Seminary," as it was called, soon enrolled 420 male and female students paying annual fees of $8 each. Ultimately separate buildings were built for female students and African American students. In 1819, the school was chartered as the "Cincinnati College" under an 1815 Ohio law. On September 26, 1821, the first commencement was held whereupon three degrees were conferred. One of those was an honorary Master of Arts degree for William Henry Harrison. A law department and medical college were later added, but during the depression of the 1820s at one point only the medical college remained open.

The Cincinnati College and the Medical College of Cincinnati ultimately survived, thanks to the tireless efforts of Daniel Drake. Drake taught medicine at the Lancaster Seminary so successfully that he was able to persuade the Ohio General Assembly to grant two charters in January 1819: one for the Cincinnati College, which the Lancaster Seminary became part of, and the other for the Medical College of Ohio. The Medical College of Cincinnati eventually became part of the University of Cincinnati, so 1819 is considered the founding date for the entire university. Drake was a professor and the president of the Medical College.

Still best known today for his dedication to healing, Drake is not as well known for his dedication to the arts and literature. However, he regularly engaged in intellectual discourses regarding politics and literature. He often held salons in his home, inviting leading authors of the day to come discuss their works with the eager Cincinnati literati. Drake also authored, or co-authored with his brother-in-law Edward Mansfield, many works, including a book called *Natural and Statistical View; Or Picture of Cincinnati and the Miami Country, Illustrated by Maps*. Mansfield described the difficulty Drake experienced as an author: ". . . his literary and scientific education, as commonly understood, terminated by necessity. Henceforward, he was . . . unable to procure a methodical course of science, till many years after his arrival at Cincinnati. In the preparation of his book he encountered, therefore, a difficulty in the want of systematized knowledge; in the want of knowing where things were to be found, and how to use them. This difficulty did not render that book, which was one of original information, less valuable to others, but it made it more laborious to himself."

Referred to as the "[Benjamin] Franklin of the West," Drake was known as one of the great leaders of intellectual thought. He regularly engaged in intellectual discourses regarding politics and literature. He often held "salons" in his home, inviting leading authors of the day to come discuss their politics and creative works with the eager Cincinnati literati.

Drake was president of a group known as the "Literary Club," whose members included his brother, Benjamin; Dr. Lyman Beecher; Beecher's daughters Harriet and Catherine; and Prof. Calvin Stowe (Harriet's husband). The cream of Cincinnati's intellectual literary crop were in the club. However, a dozen young men were not, so on October 29, 1849, they formed their own "Literary Club of Cincinnati." While Drake's group has long since dissolved, the Literary Club of Cincinnati is still growing strong in its second century.

Drake is, thankfully, less well known for the darker side of his nature. Known for airing his opinions publically, somewhat argumentative and hot-tempered, he would often stop compatriots in the street just to bicker with them if he felt the need to. Frequently friends and acquaintances would avoid his path if they saw him approaching. They weren't alone in eschewing his company.

Given Drake's strong personality, keen intellect and belief in his insight and opinions, it should be of no surprise that he often clashed with the faculty of the Medical College. One Drake biographer referred to this as the "Thirty Years War." Various battles in this "war" included Drake's being challenged to a duel (he declined) and his approaching Miami University to establish their own medical school in competition with Cincinnati's. He wrote a bitter description of the whole affair called the "Narrative of the Rise and Fall of the Medical College of Ohio."

In fact, the Medical College faculty voted in 1822 to remove him as president. They reneged in the face of public furor, but just the same Drake left for Transylvania University in Lexington, feeling unwelcome at the very college he had founded.

Drake returned to Cincinnati in 1826, hoping to establish a competing medical college in Oxford. Instead, he founded a semi-charitable institution, the Cincinnati Eye Infirmary in 1827, and did succeed in a few forays back into appointments at his Medical College of Ohio. Sadly, he died only days after accepting his last appointment there.

Drake successfully persuaded the state to grant a charter for the Commercial Hospital and Lunatic Asylum, which was built along the canal. It was the first hospital built for the pur-  pose of teaching medicine. Forty-four years after Drake's death, the Commercial Hospital and Medical College of Ohio became the University of Cincinnati's College of Medicine and General Hospital (as it was called in 1896).

Temperament aside, Daniel Drake singlehandedly left an immense footprint on the City of Cincinnati. However, healthcare is not the only area in which he left a lasting imprint. Drake had a keen interest in nature and the earth sciences, including archaeology and fossils. Through the sponsorship of six Cincinnatians and his own personal collection, they were able to open the Western Museum—now a part of the Cincinnati Museum Center. Drake donated much of his own mineral, fossil, and Native American Indian artifact collections. They looked for a curator to manage the collections and found one in John James Audubon, who was penniless and working as a taxidermist in Louisville at the time. Audubon accepted the position and worked on stuffing birds for exhibits in the museum. Audubon did not stay long, but the result of his work in Cincinnati can clearly be seen in his painstakingly correct bird illustrations, thanks in part to Drake's encouragement.

Over time, Drake owned a drugstore (the first to offer soda water), was a trustee of the city and a director of a bank, and was instrumental in founding a library, a museum, and the Lyceum. His son, Charles, also became known as a writer before moving to St. Louis and becoming a lawyer and U.S. senator. The Drake name today is still represented in the Daniel Drake Center for Post-Acute Care (a member of UC Health) and many healthcare programs.

In 1821, the Ohio State Legislature passed an act that established a "Commercial Hospital and Lunatic Asylum for the state of Ohio." So Ohio's first insane asylum was built in Cincinnati on 4 acres of land bounded on the east by the Miami & Erie Canal.

Meanwhile, immigration to the United States from Europe was increasing by leaps and bounds. By far the biggest ethnic group to enter Cincinnati from Europe was the Germans, followed at a distant second by the Irish. Suffering from the devastations of war and potato blight, Europeans looked for a fresh start in the New World, with many hoping they could find new markets for their skills.

Unfortunately, something else was still coming in from Europe: disease. Cholera had first shown up in North America from Europe in 1832, with Ohio's first cases in Cleveland. Cincinnati had been first hit in the autumn of 1832. However, cholera epidemics came in waves, by season, with the winter cold killing off the bacteria, only for the disease to reappear in the spring. One of the worst waves in Cincinnati was the cholera epidemic of 1849, with another peak in 1866.

The disease honored no ethnic or economic boundaries. Cincinnatian Harriet Beecher Stowe, author of *Uncle Tom's Cabin*, lost her infant son to cholera. After initial exposure to the bacteria, the victim quickly became ill, pale (even turning bluish), and dehydrated before finally dying within a matter of mere hours. By the time the epidemics were over, Cincinnati had lost 8,000 citizens.

Two of Cincinnati's assets turned on it at this time: its waterways. Cholera was spread by bad sanitation, and the easiest way for it to spread was by dirty water. The canal, full of filthy, stagnant water, presented a triple threat: workers in the canals were exposed to its dangers;

boats that came too close to the sides often splashed water over the berms as well as any nearby pedestrians; and children who swam in the canal were most likely ingesting the bacteria-ridden water.

But the canal was not the only watery problem contributing to the cholera epidemics. The Ohio River itself was also a contributing factor. With the poor sanitation systems, riverside industries, and the steamboats themselves, the river was not sparkling clean. Yet many people used it as a source of drinking water and for fishing, boating, and bathing.

Because the cholera outbreak had killed so many people, Cincinnati was faced with a large number of orphans. So to house the orphans, the Cincinnati Orphan Asylum was built near the corner of Twelfth and Elm Streets. Located in this same area was a potter's field, where Cincinnati Hospital buried strangers, those who committed suicide, and those who died from infectious diseases. Eventually the Over-the-Rhine area became populated enough that this practice was discontinued. But before that time, thousands of people died and needed to be buried. Often, no family members came forward to claim these people, or the entire family had died at the same time.

When Music Hall was built in 1876, construction was halted when human remains were found. According to newspaper reports at the time, some people even walked off with skulls and other bones. The city was contacted to deal with the issue but would have nothing to do with it. William Henry Harrison, who sat on the boards of both the Music Hall Association and the Spring Grove Cemetery, had all of the bones collected and re-interred in one plot.[3] It was not the last time that Music Hall renovations would uncover phantoms of the skeletal kind.

Remains were also found across Elm Street from Music Hall during Washington Park's 2012 renovation. Although these were supposed to have been relocated, not all were. One theory is that

3 http://www.spmhcincinnati.org/Music-Hall-History/Skeletons-and-Bones.php. "Bones Discovered Under Music Hall," Society for the Preservation of Music Hall, © 2014 The Society for the Preservation of Music Hall.

people feared cholera's fury and were afraid they might contract the disease by handling its victims.[4]

One of the many immigrants affected by the cholera outbreak was young Frederick Rammelsberg from Hanover, Germany, whose parents died from cholera in 1833, when Frederick was just 19. However, he didn't need the services of the Orphan Asylum as he was technically an adult. When he was 24, Frederick went into a partnership with a furniture maker named Seneca Jones. That partnership lasted only eight years, but it was not the last that Cincinnati would see of Frederick Rammelsberg.

The Commercial Hospital and Lunatic Asylum of Ohio became the parent institution for the Orphan Asylum, the City Infirmary, the Cincinnati Hospital, and Longview Asylum. Cincinnati Hospital, the main facility, was located along the canal at Twelfth and Plum Streets, which is now Twelfth Street and Central Parkway.

---

4 http://www.soapboxmedia.com/features/0329graypapecincinnati.aspx. Steven Rosen, "Digging Up the Past for Future Development," *Soapbox*, March 29, 2011.

CHAPTER 6

WE'VE GOT THE GOODS

AT THE TURN OF THE NINETEENTH CENTURY, an English candlemaker named William Procter had immigrated with his wife to the United States after his London dry-goods shop was robbed. Alas, his wife did not fare well on the trip, becoming ill and dying soon after their arrival in Cincinnati. Procter, however, found a good home here. He obtained work at a bank while he pursued his craft on the side. His skills at making candles were perfectly suited for the tallow and fat by-products produced by "Porkopolis." His candlemaking thrived, enabling him to pay off the debt incurred through the robbery of his store. Soon he quit the day job he held at a bank and turned to making candles full time. He also began keeping company with a young lady by the name of Olivia Norris, the daughter of Alexander Norris.

Two years Procter's junior, James Gamble was following a similar path. His family also faced challenges in the newly formed United Kingdom, but in Ireland. In 1819, facing overpopulation, a major depression, and rampant disease following the Napoleonic Wars, many Irish decided to go to the United States—the Gamble family among them. However, 16-year-old James became ill en route, forcing the family to stop in Cincinnati before reaching their intended destination of Illinois. By the time James had recovered, the family had grown attached to Cincinnati and put down roots.

James apprenticed himself to a man who made soaps and candles, eventually becoming a soap and candlemaker himself. He married Elizabeth Ann Norris, thus becoming a brother-in-law to William Procter. Their father-in-law, Alexander, noted that the two were competing against each other for resources and began his campaign to get the two to become partners. After years of persuasion, he finally succeeded.

William Procter and James Gamble signed the partnership agreement on October 31, 1837, thus establishing the Procter & Gamble Company. Their total assets were $7,192.24: just a little less than the value of what had been stolen from Procter's London shop.

They began by creating soaps and candles for Cincinnati's citizenry. Gamble made the soaps and candles, and Procter took care of administrative duties and marketing. He loaded the products up in their wheelbarrow and carted them around to the various stores to sell. Soon their business grew enough that they could move to a location on Western Row (now called Central Avenue), closer to the slaughterhouses.

They were not alone in taking advantage of the rich supply of pork fats, though. By the end of the decade, they were joined by Michael Werk from Alsace, Thomas Emery from England, and Andrew Jergens from Germany, all of whom started businesses using the abundant fats and oils of Porkopolis to make soaps and candles. Soon Cincinnati's soaps were sold throughout the state, thanks to a great extent to the canals.

Thomas Emery did not always enjoy success in his candlemaking. Born in England, he immigrated to the United States in 1832 with his wife and his son, Thomas Josephus Emery. Emery first tried his hand at selling real estate and then began dabbling in soaps and lard oil. His first attempts only landed him in bankruptcy, however. Soon enough, Thomas Emery found his niche: real estate and fatty acids.

Through the city's rail lines and the Ohio River, Cincinnati had access to the South and its great variety of trees, such as cherry and walnut, and the oaks of the Midwest, as well as evergreens from the North and imported mahogany. An oak blight in England placed furniture from the United States in high demand. At one point more than 150 furniture factories could be found in Cincinnati and its environs.

Cincinnati furniture makers embraced the steam-powered machines and saws used to increase production and make quick work of the larger pieces of timber. Then woodworkers, inlayers, and carvers focused on completing the intricate details of custom inlay and design by hand. By the 1840s, Cincinnati had become a mecca for furniture manufacturing in the Unites States.

For young Frederick Rammelsberg, Cincinnati's location meant a personal boon to his furniture business. In 1846 he entered into a new partnership with Irishman Robert Mitchell, whom he had met at his boarding house. Their company got off to a rocky start when an 1848 fire totally wiped them out. They were uninsured, but they managed to rebuild.

While they were building their business, they were also building their families. Frederick married Sarah Maria Lape in 1842 and had eight children with her (seven of whom lived to adulthood). Robert, who had married Harriet Hannaford in 1838, had eight children. Four of these survived infancy: two daughters and

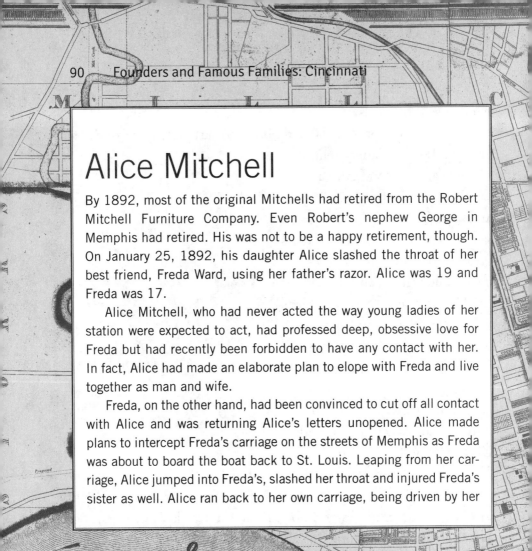

Alice Mitchell

By 1892, most of the original Mitchells had retired from the Robert Mitchell Furniture Company. Even Robert's nephew George in Memphis had retired. His was not to be a happy retirement, though. On January 25, 1892, his daughter Alice slashed the throat of her best friend, Freda Ward, using her father's razor. Alice was 19 and Freda was 17.

Alice Mitchell, who had never acted the way young ladies of her station were expected to act, had professed deep, obsessive love for Freda but had recently been forbidden to have any contact with her. In fact, Alice had made an elaborate plan to elope with Freda and live together as man and wife.

Freda, on the other hand, had been convinced to cut off all contact with Alice and was returning Alice's letters unopened. Alice made plans to intercept Freda's carriage on the streets of Memphis as Freda was about to board the boat back to St. Louis. Leaping from her carriage, Alice jumped into Freda's, slashed her throat and injured Freda's sister as well. Alice ran back to her own carriage, being driven by her

two sons. He married again in 1863, this time to a woman named Lucinda, with a grown daughter named A. Lida.

Rammelsberg and Mitchell took advantage of the great variety and quantity of lumber from the South and the multiple means of transportation via canal, river, and road, and built a furniture empire. With fire obviously being a major concern to furniture manufacturers, Rammelsberg and Mitchell moved their company to Fourth Street (where many will remember McAlpin's being later in the twentieth century), and spread their operations out over six floors. Having their company wiped out in their second year of

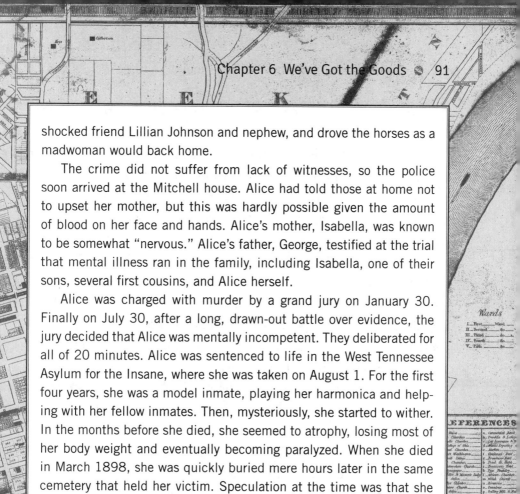

shocked friend Lillian Johnson and nephew, and drove the horses as a madwoman would back home.

The crime did not suffer from lack of witnesses, so the police soon arrived at the Mitchell house. Alice had told those at home not to upset her mother, but this was hardly possible given the amount of blood on her face and hands. Alice's mother, Isabella, was known to be somewhat "nervous." Alice's father, George, testified at the trial that mental illness ran in the family, including Isabella, one of their sons, several first cousins, and Alice herself.

Alice was charged with murder by a grand jury on January 30. Finally on July 30, after a long, drawn-out battle over evidence, the jury decided that Alice was mentally incompetent. They deliberated for all of 20 minutes. Alice was sentenced to life in the West Tennessee Asylum for the Insane, where she was taken on August 1. For the first four years, she was a model inmate, playing her harmonica and helping with her fellow inmates. Then, mysteriously, she started to wither. In the months before she died, she seemed to atrophy, losing most of her body weight and eventually becoming paralyzed. When she died in March 1898, she was quickly buried mere hours later in the same cemetery that held her victim. Speculation at the time was that she died from tuberculosis, or "consumption" as it was called then.

business, they weren't about to endure that again. The furniture, as well as the raw materials for manufacturing, were better separated so that a fire would not spread as easily. Each floor had a different display for the customer to see what the furniture looked like in a homelike setting.

The company grew like gangbusters, selling furniture to residential customers as well as to steamboat companies, to outfit the cabins. Their residential products included a large inventory of readily available machined, inexpensive furniture as well as the hand-finished, craftsman furniture that was available only by special order.

The company was to become the largest furniture company in the United States.

Success didn't last long for furniture king Frederick Rammelsberg, unfortunately. Rammelsberg died young on January 30, 1863, at the age of 49. Although Rammelsberg's partner, Robert Mitchell, bought out all of Rammelsberg's shares and took over the reins of the company at that point, Mitchell waited until 1881 to change the name to Robert Mitchell Furniture Company. His brothers, John and William, joined him in the business. William opened a showroom store in St. Louis that sold Mitchell Furniture, but did not manufacture it. John opened a store in Memphis under the name of Mitchell, Hoffman & Company. Robert's sons, Richard and Albert, joined their father in the family business.

During the influx of Europeans before the Civil War, two brothers arrived in Cincinnati: Maximilian and Charles Louis Fleischmann. The Fleischmanns were originally from what is now known as the Czech Republic. There, Charles had managed a Vienna distillery where he produced spirits and baked goods.

When they arrived in Cincinnati, they immediately set to work to continue their trade here. However, they were disappointed in the quality of yeast here, so they returned to Austria for European yeast. They developed a way to make compressed yeast from a by-product of distilling rye whisky that had been considered waste. They also invented and patented a machine for distillation. With James Graff's financial support, they opened the Vienna Model Bakery. Their renown grew for their yeast and distillation prowess.

Besides his forays into baking and distilling, Charles was also exceedingly successful in politics. He served two terms in the Ohio senate and was an aide to William McKinley while the latter was governor of Ohio. This affinity for politics would be shared later by his son, Julius.

On September 1, 1890, Maximilian Fleischmann died. He left behind a yeast and distilling dynasty. He also left behind a will that grew into a legal quagmire.

On December 10, 1897, his brother Charles Fleischmann died suddenly from natural causes. It was a loss felt by many in both Cincinnati and in New York City. His obituary in the *New York Times* said, "His charities were constant and splendid. It is said of him that he never denied an appeal for help, and he gave quickly and with his heart in what his hand did. He was popular everywhere among all conditions of men. . . . He was always pleasant, affable, kindly, just, and honest. He was not only liked, but implicitly trusted."

That was not to remain the case. The guardian of Maximilian's infant children brought suit in New York court against Charles Fleischmann (deceased), his sons Julius, Max C., and Louis, and Maximilian's widow, Johanna, over the handling of Fleischmann & Co. upon the death of Maximilian. Johanna was both a plaintiff and a defendant in the case. Julius had just been elected Cincinnati's mayor (its youngest ever). As a result of the lawsuit, all the books of the Cincinnati branch of the company had to be taken to New York to be evaluated. It proved to be a very sticky mess for the heirs of the yeast baron.

The twentieth century dawned in Cincinnati with little with little inclination of the issues would tear the city apart over the next 40 years: anti-German sentiment, Prohibition, cholera, the Great Depression, and others. In 1901, distiller Julius Fleischmann was elected mayor, at 29 the youngest to ever hold that post (up to that time and since). He had broad support from many groups: the Germans liked his liberal stance on liquor; the Protestants, Jews, and Catholics liked his philanthropic donations to many charities; and many appreciated him as part-owner of the Cincinnati Reds. Julius served as mayor until 1905. He and his brother Max continued to support their brother-in-law, Christian Holmes, in his quest to build a sanitary, modern private hospital.

The air in the neighborhood of St. Bernard today carries a certain scent of success. Over the years, it has been home to many companies (like P&G, Fries and Fries, and National Distillers) whose products have a distinct aroma. Many passersby on the highway probably find these smells pleasing, whether soap, food flavorings or alcohol. In the

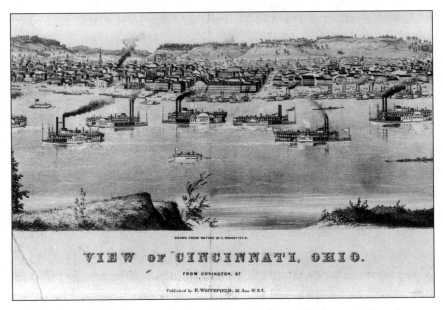

VIEW OF CINCINNATI, OHIO.

FROM COVINGTON, KY

Published by E. WHITEFIELD, 32 Ann St N.Y.

In 1848, health concerns were beginning to plague the burgeoning city in the form of air pollution from its industries and disease carried by its waterways.

Credit: Drawn by E. Whitefield, Library of Congress

nineteenth century, however, before the advent of such regulatory bodies as the Environmental Protection Agency, some of the smells in the air were not so pleasant. Thomas Emery's lard oil factory on Water Street, for example, was said to emit bitter odors so strong that the homes were continually pervaded with the smells.

Emery's business boomed by the mid-1840s, but Emery didn't live long past that to enjoy it. He fell through a hatch in his own factory and died in 1857. The trustees of his estate soon recognized that Emery's oldest two sons, Thomas Josephus and John Josiah—then in their 20s—were better suited to run their father's business than they. Emery had also had another son, J. Howard, and two daughters, Julia and Kezia, but they didn't take an active role in the business as did Thomas and John.

Meanwhile, interesting developments were taking place at Emery's competition, Procter & Gamble. Because of the invention of the electric light bulb, candle sales had fallen off. Before the war started, William Procter and James Gamble feared that their supply of rosin from the south might be cut off. (Rosin, used in many industries, is frequently obtained from the resin or sap of southern pine trees.) They sent their sons, cousins James Norris Gamble and William Alexander Procter, to the south to buy up as much rosin as they could. Three months after their purchase, war broke out and Procter & Gamble was sitting on the largest supply of rosin. Thus, with the Civil War came profitable government contracts for soap, so business was booming at P&G.

Then as the 1870s came to a close, a worker at Procter & Gamble had a happy accident. It is said that he went to lunch, leaving the blending machine running on a batch of white soap. The result was a batch of hard soap that could float. The customers who received the floating soap loved it and wanted more. Harley Procter, son of founder William Procter, wanted to market it separately from their regular white soap, however. He reported that he was sitting in church and read Psalm 45:8: "All thy garments smell of myrrh, and aloes, and cassia, out of the ivory palaces, whereby they have made thee glad." Suddenly he had his name for the new soap: Ivory!

The 1870s brought one of the worst financial panics to hit the country, with the failure of the bank Jay Cooke and Company, which had funded the Northern Pacific Railroad. By the time the country recovered, about five years later, thousands of businesses had failed, including many banks and railroads. But at least one business got its start in all this tragedy.

Bernard Henry Kroger's father was an immigrant from Germany who ran a dry goods store in Covington, Kentucky, just over the river from Cincinnati. The Financial Panic of 1873 cost him everything he had—including his life—so his 13-year-old son, Barney (as he was known), began working to help the family of 12 to make ends meet. Barney's jobs didn't meet with his mother's approval (because he had to work on the Sabbath), until he found himself working for the Great Northern and Pacific Tea Company, selling coffee and tea door-to-door. It was a sign of things to come.

Among Cincinnati's premiere companies, Procter & Gamble led the way in considering the well-being of its workers and in looking out for their welfare as employees rather than as replaceable resources. In 1886, they cut Saturdays to a half-day of work for their factory workers. In 1887, they started offering an employee profit-sharing plan, followed closely by pensions and disability benefits. This would not be the last time that P&G set a precedent that other companies followed.

At this time, William A. Procter (son of P&G co-founder William Procter) was serving on the board of trustees of the University of Cincinnati in addition to carrying out his duties to the family business. While a UC trustee, he felt it to be his personal charge to build a formidable library collection. Anticipating the opening of the new Van Wormer Library on the new Burnet Woods campus, he began buying up private libraries and collections and donating them to the university. His foundation of more than 8,200 books gave the University Libraries their head start on what is today a collection of more than 4 million volumes.

Barney Kroger had found his talent in food retail and soon worked his way up into management, finally owning his own store. He and a friend, B. A. Branagan, established the Great Western Tea Company in 1883 when Kroger was only 23. Misfortune arrived in their first year, however, in the form of an accident between a train and their new horse and cart, with Branagan at the reins. Branagan lived to tell about it, but the cart and horse were a total loss. Then one of Cincinnati's many floods destroyed their inventory—another total loss. Nevertheless, they turned a profit by the end of their first year, and Kroger was able to buy out Branagan's share. In 1884 Barney Kroger bought a second store.

Just as Kroger's youth had been affected by a financial panic, another panic had a profound effect on his career. When the Panic of 1893 hit, Kroger felt sure that his bank would not fail. He left his money in the bank. As many businesses around him folded, he bought them up. By the end of the crisis, he owned 17 stores. By the end of the century, he would change how consumers shopped. He bought items in bulk, which could then be sold at his numerous stores. He would also soon begin to offer in-store baked goods and butcher shops. For the first time anywhere, Barney was offering shoppers lower prices and convenience.

By the twentieth century, it had become quite evident that Barney Kroger was a successful food retailer. What was less well known was that he was also a generous benefactor, often making magnanimous donations yet specifically seeking anonymity. For example, he asked a *Cincinnati Post* journalist to bring him someone who was in financial distress. The reporter brought him a young doctor who was working with tuberculosis patients; Kroger gave him $6,000. In 1911 Kroger worked with Frances Pollak and others to establish the Cincinnati Association for the Blind to help those with visual disabilities get access to assistance, job training, and education.

Similar to how William Procter, James Gamble, and Michael Werk had found Cincinnati a fertile ground for soap and candle production earlier in the century, German immigrant Andrew Jergens took the plunge in 1881 by investing his life's savings in a soap company owned by Charles H. Geilfus. The newly renamed Western Soap Company first emerged in 1882; after Jergens and Geilfus were joined by Jergens's brothers Al and Herman, it became known as the Andrew Jergens Company. They located their factory near the slaughterhouses—the major source for their products. But one thing that set their soaps apart from those of the competition was that they used coconut oil as an ingredient.

Andrew N. Jergens was born in 1881—another landmark for the Jergens family. He often said that he went to work for the family business at the age of 11, working from the bottom up. He worked for the Andrew Jergens Company until his death at the age of 86 in 1967.

In 1962, while he was president of the family company, Andrew N. Jergens established the Andrew Jergens Foundation, a philanthropic foundation for charitable works in the city of Cincinnati. Separate from the Andrew Jergens Company (which has changed hands and is now a wholly owned subsidiary of the Kao Corporation), the foundation recently celebrated its 50th anniversary and the $17 million it has given away in grants in the areas of social services, health, recreation/environment, arts, and education. Andrew Jergens's grandchildren and great-grandchildren serve on the board of trustees.

A health concern was troubling the nation, and it was one in which Cincinnati would play a leading role. Health laws required testing of raw milk; some dairies tested both raw and pasteurized milk. In the late 1800s and early 1900s, the purity of milk was paramount. In fact, Cincinnati played a role in the national movement for milk purity.

In 1906, physicians in Cincinnati established a milk commission, which called for a national conference to be held on June 3, 1907, in Atlantic City. The Atlantic City meeting established the American Association of Medical Milk Commissions. One concern of the association was the number of infants who died from severe diarrhea, or "summer complaint" (identified also in historical documents as being cholera or severe gastroenteritis). "Summer complaint" sounds trivial, but its effects were deadly. Doctors often pointed their fingers at milk that had not been kept cool while riding around on milk wagons during delivery. The problem wouldn't be solved right away, but it was a group of Cincinnatians once again who came up with the solution.

The early 1920s dealt a personal blow to two of Cincinnati's greatest families. In 1923, while playing in the traditional Thanksgiving football game between Miami University and the University of Cincinnati, James Gamble Nippert was injured. Nippert, son of Judge Alfred K. and Maud Gamble Nippert, had graduated from Culver Military Academy in Indiana and had returned to UC for a law degree, after serving in the Army at the end of World War I. He played football for a while, but then left the team to focus on his law studies. His cleats were filled by his younger brother, Louis, but never quite as well. Jimmy came back to the team at center. The team was beginning to win more games when they went into their final game of the season against their local rivals.

After a pregame chicken race, the game began. In the third quarter, Nippert was stepped on by one of the Miami players, but he stayed in the game. Despite Nippert's injury, the nasty, sloppy field, and the rainy weather, UC won, 23-0. However, Nippert's wound got worse, turning septic—some say as a result of the chicken droppings on the field. In December he was taken from his home in Westwood to the Christ Hospital. Ironically, Christ Hospital had been founded by his grandfather, in honor of Jimmy's great-grandmother, Elizabeth Gamble.

For 12 days Jimmy Nippert's mother did not leave his side. She sent a message to the UC students via the *News Record*, the student newspaper, giving them an update and saying that her son thanked them for their interest. Despite the well wishes of the entire campus, on Christmas morning, Nippert uttered, "Five more yards to go, then drop"—the last words he had spoken during the game—and then died in his mother's arms. He was 23.

In his memory, Nippert's grandfather James N. Gamble (a partner at P&G) donated the funds to build a new stadium. Dedicated September 27, 1924, Nippert Stadium is currently the fifth-oldest stadium in college football.

The great flood of 1937, which crested at 80 feet, changed Cincinnati in many ways forever. Because of Cincinnati's natural plateau, the floodwaters never advanced north of Fourth Street. Some businesses, having survived the Great Depression, could not overcome a second blow and were forced to close. During the flood of 1937, the Roebling Suspension Bridge was the only bridge still above water; it had been built high enough to for the steamboats' stacks to pass safely below it.

Prior to the flood, Front Street had been home to many produce wholesalers—as depicted in the movie *The Pride of Jesse Hallam* (written by Ohio resident Suzanne Clauser). Some of these families found themselves moving multiple times, and not just for flood-waters. For example, the Sam Caruso Fruit and Vegetable Company was founded in 1932 on West Court Street. They merged with the Ciresi Bros. and moved to Front and Vine Streets down by the river.

Another flood in 1997, which crested at 65 feet, also closed businesses and moved others. The Children's Museum was forced to close. It eventually moved from Longworth Hall to be part of the Cincinnati Museum Center at Union Terminal. The Old Spaghetti Factory Restaurant closed because of water damage, but then reopened in Fairfield, Ohio, about 20 miles north of Cincinnati.

But it was not the water that made the merged company move: it was ball games. "What kind?" you might ask. Well, in 1968 Caruso-Ciresi had to move to get out of the way for Riverfront Stadium, then 30 years later had to move again to make room for Paul Brown Stadium.

Although Cincinnatians were hit by the Great Depression, many say it was not as bad here as elsewhere in the country. Some say it was because of Cincinnatians' conservative approach to money. (This might have been true; however, many Cincinnatians were hurt badly in the savings and loan debacle of the 1990s, perhaps because those conservative Cincinnatians were letting their money sit in passbook accounts.)

During the Depression, people would get nervous about their money in the bank, then they would run to the bank and withdraw everything. However, banks don't have everyone's money inside the bank at any one time; the money is out being used in the form of loans so that it can earn interest. If all the customers were to demand their money back at the same time, the bank could not provide it.

One day in 1933, Provident Bank's customers were getting skittish. They descended upon the bank in great numbers, demanding their money. Barney Kroger was Provident's chairman of the Board of Trustees at the time. He immediately took several million dollars in bonds from his own safe deposit box and guaranteed a loan of currency from the Federal Reserve Bank, secured with his own money. He then directed the employees of the bank to line the windows with stacks of cash. Any of the bank's customers who still wanted their money had to form a single-file line past the stacks of money while Kroger waved handfuls of bank notes at them, assuring them of the safety of their money. Suitably reassured, most of the people left their money in Provident and left the bank for home.

Barney Kroger no longer owned his company at this time, incidentally. In 1928—long before the stock market crash of 1929—he had sold his interest in the 5,575-store company for $28 million. After the Depression, though, since he survived with his fortune intact, he bought back a third of the company to show his confidence in the company and to help it rebuild.

Barney Kroger supported many Cincinnati institutions and causes, often without fanfare or credit. He donated five Bengal tigers to the Cincinnati zoo, for example, and funded tuberculosis research. He died in 1938 at the age of 78.

In the late 1930s, most milk was delivered directly to the homes. As the milkmen went around to their customers, each customer would indicate how many bottles she wanted that day. In those days, often if the mistress of the house was not home, the milkman would put the milk in her icebox for her.

During 1932–36, most local dairies phased out their horse-drawn milk wagons and turned to motorized vehicles to make home deliveries. It was unusual for a delivery truck to sell all of its milk. "Returned milk" was that milk left over in the truck after the day's deliveries. Therefore, the milk that came back had to be tested to see if it was still suitable for use. One of the uses for returns was to separate out the fat and make butter with it. Most of the time, the milk had to be discarded.

Carl Henry Lindner, along with his three sons and daughter (Carl, Robert, Richard, and Dorothy), made his mark on the Cincinnati

(continued on page 106)

The Cincinnati Zoo & Botanical Garden: A Tale of Two Birdies

(And Hundreds of English Sparrows)

In the mid- to late-nineteenth century, Cincinnati had a caterpillar problem. It seems the local birds were falling down on the job of getting rid of the intruding insects, so in 1872, Andrew Erkenbrecher and a handful of other businessmen got an ingenious idea. If our local birds were looking down their beaks at the idea of eating these marauding creatures, then they would bring in some foreign birds to do the job for them. They dispatched to Europe for a collection of birds, including starlings and English sparrows (which, as it turns out, are neither English nor sparrows; they're finches), to take care of the growing caterpillar problem.

They also fed the birds, which would seem to defeat the purpose of why they were brought here, but nevertheless they provided the birds with room and board. So birds did what birds do and they multiplied. Erkenbrecher housed the birds in Burnet Woods, calling it the "Society for the Acclimatization of Birds."

Cities worldwide such as Moscow, London, and Berlin followed Cincinnati's example. The "Acclimatization Society of Cincinnati" was formed in 1873 to assist in these efforts. Much to the chagrin of future Cincinnatians, Erkenbrecher *et al* released their birds to the wild. English (or more accurately, "house") sparrows are exotic species. They act like invaders, frequently taking over the nesting cavities of similar domestic species, often destroying the eggs or even attacking the adults. European starlings are now the most abundant songbird in the United States.

But showing some foresight, Erkenbrecher formed the Zoological Society of Cincinnati in 1873. A site of 66½ acres near the center of Cincinnati (known as Blakely Woods) was leased in 1874 for the site of the zoo. Finally in 1875, the zoo officially opened on September 18. It was the second zoo in the country, just over a year behind Philadelphia's.

The initial collection was small, compared to today's: more than 400 birds (probably mostly English sparrows and starlings), eight monkeys, six raccoons, three deer, two grizzly bears, two elk, a buffalo, a hyena, a tiger, a circus elephant, and an alligator. At least one of the birds was a talking crow.

Since then, the zoo has had many important—even *nationally* significant—milestones. Here are just a few:

1875: The zoo opened its doors, charging 25 cents for adults and 15 cents for children.

1877: An Indian rhinoceros and California sea lion exhibit were added.

1878: A sea lion was born—the first ever born in captivity. The zoo acquired a pair of giraffes: Daisy and Abe.

1880: The zoo celebrated the first trumpeter swan ever born in captivity and the birth of four passenger pigeons.

1882: The first American bison was born in captivity.

1886: Faced with rising debt, zoo management sold 22 acres to stay afloat.

1888: The zoo acquired Mr. and Mrs. Rooney, thought to be the only captive chimpanzees in the nation at the time.

1898: The zoo went into receivership because of its debts and the effects of the Depression of 1893–1898.

1899: The Cincinnati Zoological Company organized to operate on a nonprofit basis.

1901: The Cincinnati Traction Company bought controlling stock to run the zoo on a nonprofit basis.

1903: The zoo opened a three-acre buffalo range.

1906: The Elephant House opened.

1914: The world's last surviving passenger pigeon, Martha, died. Her body was immediately frozen and shipped to the Smithsonian Institution in Washington, D.C.

1917: Anna Sinton (Mrs. Charles Phelps) Taft and Mary Emery bought the zoo for $250,000.

1918: The world's last surviving Carolina parakeet, Incas, died.

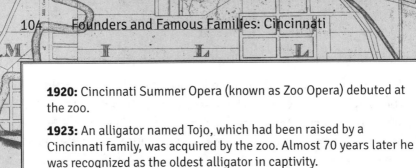

1920: Cincinnati Summer Opera (known as Zoo Opera) debuted at the zoo.

1923: An alligator named Tojo, which had been raised by a Cincinnati family, was acquired by the zoo. Almost 70 years later he was recognized as the oldest alligator in captivity.

1931: The zoo acquired Susie, its first gorilla.

1932: The zoo was formally transferred to the city of Cincinnati for $325,000. The zoo was incorporated as the Zoological Society of Cincinnati. The City's Board of Park Commissioners took over operations.

1937: The Reptile House opened. It was converted into the Bird House in 1951.

1938: The Children's Zoo opened.

1947: Susie, the zoo's most popular attraction, died. At 22 she was then the oldest gorilla in captivity.

1952: King Tut, patriarch of the zoo's gorilla family, arrived.

1957: Dr. Albert Schweitzer donated a 3-year-old gorilla named Penelope to the children of Cincinnati; she was later given to the zoo.

1970: Sam was the first gorilla born at the zoo; eight days later, Samantha was born.

1971: Opera left the zoo, after 51 years, for Music Hall.

1974: The Gibbon Islands exhibit opened. The Zoo's Education Department opened. *Newsweek* magazine called the Cincinnati Zoo the sexiest zoo in the country for its successful breeding practices such as holding the record for gorilla births, black rhino births, and being one of only five zoos in the world to breed Komodo dragons.

1975: Big Cat Canyon opened with three 1-year-old white tigers. The Elephant House, Reptile House, and Aviary House were listed on the National Register of Historic Places.

1977: The last original Aviary building was relocated and opened as the Passenger Pigeon Memorial building.

1981: The Research Department opened and the first artificial insemination of an exotic feline species (Persian leopard) successfully occurred.

1982: The zoo opened a cryogenics unit and began freezing and storing embryos, eggs, and semen. The zoo was given the 100-acre Anna Mast Farm for breeding.

1985: Carnivora House was renovated and renamed the "Cat House." Red Panda exhibit opened, and the renovated Monkey Island opened.

1987: The Cincinnati Zoological Garden was renamed the Cincinnati Zoo and Botanical Garden; the zoo was designated a National Historic Landmark.

1989: The first banded linsang born in captivity in the United States was born in the Cincinnati Zoo.

1990: The Komodo Dragon exhibit opened, and the Botanical Center and Oriental Garden opened.

1991: The Carl H. Lindner Center for the Reproduction of Endangered Wildlife (CREW) was dedicated.

1995: The zoo set a U.S. record with six gorilla births in one year, including the world's first test-tube gorilla.

2011: Cincinnati celebrated the birth, then mourned the death three months later, of Zuri the giraffe.

2012: Sarah, an 11-year-old cheetah, set a new record for the fastest land mammal by running the 100-meter dash in 5.95 seconds. She accomplished this feat while filming for a *National Geographic* magazine shoot. Her top speed was 61 mph.

2012: The city mourned the death of Ipuh, a 33-year-old Sumatran rhino, believed to be the oldest such rhino in captivity. Giraffe lovers were heartened by the birth of another baby Masai giraffe, Lulu.

2013: Cincinnati Zoo was chosen as the ideal home for baby Gladys, a Western Lowland gorilla, who was born in January 2013 but who was rejected by her mother. A team of 10 human surrogate "mothers" wearing special furs worked around the clock to assist in Gladys's "gorillification" until she could make the transition to a real gorilla surrogate.

On April 16, 2008, Cincinnati Zoo Executive Director and former UC President Nancy Zimpher held a press conference to announce that the zoo had obtained a new baby binturong—or "bearcat." Later named Lucy, to match the zoo's aging binturong, Ricky, the little critter became a popular sight on the sidelines of UC's football games (except she's not so little anymore).

Credit: Lisa Ventre/UC Photo Services

(continued from page 101)

dairy world in 1938 by offering dairy products on a "cash-and-carry" basis in his store in Norwood. Because he had no delivery costs, he could offer his milk and dairy products at discounted prices.

Furthermore, because his milk was not being carried around on milk wagons all day, less milk was spoiled, which again reduced costs. Of course, part of the challenge was convincing housewives that the lower-priced, cold milk was worth the effort to go to the store to get it.

Their sales on the first day of business amounted to an underwhelming $8.28. Even worse, when Lindner senior closed up the store that night, two milkmen—upset at the competition their wagons would face—met him at the back door and worked him over.

Some of Cincinnati's biggest movers and shakers move some dirt at the groundbreaking for UC's Richard E. Lindner Varsity Village: Sandy Heimann, Jeff Wyler, Bob Goins, former UC President Joseph Steger, George Schaeffer, Richard Lindner, Carl Lindner, and C. Francis Barrett. Photo taken May 6, 2003.

Credit: University of Cincinnati Photo Services

Still, the Lindners were not to be scared off. United Dairy Farmers was in the milk business for good.

In the early 1950s, as Carl Lindner's health got worse, Carl Jr. stepped in to take over the management of United Dairy Farmers (UDF). When Carl Lindner (senior) died in 1952, they had 11 stores. By 1958, Cincinnati was home to 22 stores. Not bad for someone who never finished high school!

Eventually Carl Lindner Jr. left the running of UDF to his younger brother Robert while he turned his attention to American Financial Corp., a holding company he had created in 1959. Slowly but surely, Carl Lindner Jr. started acquiring other businesses, both local and international. The Lindner empire at one point included Great American Insurance Co., Provident Financial Group, Chiquita

(continued on page 110)

It's ~~Greek~~ ^Macedonian to Me

Ask most people who have eaten in Cincinnati to name three iconic Cincinnati foods and its chili is sure to be among them. Cincinnati chili is not like chili you'll find anywhere else: no fiery hot jalapenos or habaneros, no chunks of beef, no hints of hot sauce or colorful flashes of diced bell peppers. Instead—depending on which parlor you're patronizing—you'll get hints of allspice, garlic, and cumin. Some swear they taste cinnamon, cocoa, and Worcestershire sauce, even.

And Cincinnati chili is served on spaghetti. "It's Greek," some polite Cincinnatian will explain to a newbie.

But that's not completely correct. If you go to Greece, you might find stews with the flavors that resemble Cincinnati's chili, but nothing called "chili" with cheese on the top and spaghetti on the bottom. And none of this "three-way, four-way, or five-way" stuff. That was invented by the folks at Empress Chili, which is the home of what is now known as "Cincinnati chili."

Brothers Tom and John Kiradjieff emigrated from what we now know as the Republic of Macedonia (just north of Greece) and ended up in Cincinnati. In 1922, they opened up what was originally just a hot dog shop in the burlesque theatre on Vine Street between Eighth and Ninth Streets, downtown. Originally called the Gaiety Theatre, the theatre was now called the Empress.

The Kiradjieff brothers' plan was to serve Greek food in addition to the hot dogs, but their home cooking was not finding a wide audience. So to appeal to their very German clientele, they made up a recipe that was reminiscent of the flavors of their homeland, then they doctored it.

"They added a dozen spices like chili, plus garlic and onions, and ground beef," says Tom's son, Joe. Then the brothers served the concoction steaming hot over spaghetti. It was a big hit. They called themselves "Empress Chili," after the burlesque theatre. Evidently it made a good landmark.

The Kiradjieffs also came up with the three-way, four-way, and five-way concept. A three-way is spaghetti, chili, and cheese. A four-way adds beans or onions. A five-way adds both. They served a plate with a couple of hot dogs on the side with some steaming chili and cheese on top (now known as "Coneys").

Tom's son, Joe, operated the Empress empire starting in the 1950s after his father's health declined. Joe retired in 2009, after selling Empress to another chili family.

In 1928, a young, Greek Empress employee named Nicholas Sarakatsannis went South (literally, not figuratively). He went to Northern Kentucky. Sarakatsannis had come to Cincinnati from Dayton with his wife and children. He had stopped in the Empress Chili parlor looking for a job and was immediately put to work. Within short order, he felt he could come up with a better recipe, but didn't want to compete directly with the Kiradjieffs, so he crossed the river. Thus Dixie Chili was born in Newport, where it still operates today just north of Eighth Street. It has since expanded in many ways. It has three locations, many food offerings, and a six-way! The six-way is composed of chili, spaghetti, beans, onions, fresh garlic, and cheese.

Another Greek Nicholas got his start with the Kiradjieffs also: Nicholas Lambrinides. Like young Sarakatsannis, Lambrinides got the itch to open his own chili parlor, so he headed for the hills: Price Hill, specifically. In 1949, he and three of his sons opened the first Skyline Chili parlor at the intersection of Glenway and Quebec Avenues. The original parlor has since been demolished, but you can find plenty of other Skylines throughout Cincinnati and as far away as Naples, Florida.

Meanwhile, in 1940, a single chili parlor quietly opened in Camp Washington. In 1951, Greek immigrant Johnny Johnson, now the Johnson family patriarch, started working at Camp Washington Chili and he's never worked anywhere else. Although they had to move back a little because of a widening of the street, they've always been right where they are now: Hopple Street off of I-75.

Featured on Travel Channel's *Man vs. Food,* they have won numerous awards, including a James Beard award in 2000. In 2013, *Smithsonian Magazine* named them one of its "20 Most Iconic Food Destinations Across America."

It was Johnny Johnson's son-in-law, Joe Papakirk, who bought Empress Chili from Joe Kiradjieff in 2009. If you can't beat 'em, buy 'em!

Although Cincinnati is home to almost 200 chili parlors, the biggest contenders for Greater Cincinnati's favorite chili typically boil down to Empress, Skyline, Dixie, Camp Washington, and Gold Star (started by four Jordanian brothers). Which one is best is a big debate in Cincinnati that will surely never be settled.

One thing that most Cincinnatians agree on, though, is that when eating a plate of chili spaghetti, you don't twirl it, you cut into it so that you get all the layers in each bite. No matter how many ways you slice it, "Greek" chili is definitely an All-American family favorite in Cincinnati.

Carl (left) and Richard Lindner shake hands with Bob Goins, then UC Athletic Director, at the May 12, 2006, dedication and opening of UC's Richard E. Lindner Varsity Village.

Credit: Andrew Higley/UC Photo Services

(continued from page 107)

Brands, the Cincinnati Reds, the *Cincinnati Enquirer,* Thriftway, and Bantam Books, among others.

The Lindner family's generosity reached far as well. Carl was a generous supporter of the Cincinnati Pops Orchestra, the Cincinnati Zoo's Center for Reproduction of Endangered Wildlife ("CREW"), and the Ice Age Exhibit at the Cincinnati Museum Center. Brother Robert supported the Robert D. Lindner Family Omnimax Theater, also at the Cincinnati Museum Center. Richard Lindner's sponsorship created the Richard E. Lindner Varsity Village on the University of Cincinnati Uptown Campus. In 1989 Carl Lindner and his second wife, Edyth, founded a school, Cincinnati Hills Christian Academy, which has become one of the leading private Christian K–12 schools in the area.

Cincinnati's Confectionary Families

Cincinnatians love their food. Thanks to the city's many German and Greek immigrants, when one thinks of Cincinnati over the years, many restaurants come to mind and perhaps a touch of drool escapes from the mouth, even. Ah! But what about dessert? Cincinnati is famous for its "Chili wars"—hotly contested battles between Skyline, Gold Star, and other chili parlors and their patrons over whose chili is best. Well, a frosty war wages at the other end of the meal in a bitter battle for the title of best sweets of the Queen City.

This confectionary contention has gone on for "more than a hundred years," as *Cincinnati Enquirer* food reviewer Polly Campbell put it in response to chef Michael Symon's "Food Feud" television show. Symon, a Cleveland native, attempted to answer the question that has burned in the minds and palates of Cincinnatians for decades: whose chocolate chip ice cream is better—Graeter's or Aglamesis Brothers'? Well, in the show, Graeter's ice cream won, but "Ags" fans say that proves nothing, that people were blinded by the large chips (which are mostly just a function of stirring speed and the type of fat in the chocolate).

Meanwhile, Graeter's and Aglamesis (pronounced "a-glah-MEE-siss," *not* "a-gluh-MEE-seez") Brothers are not the only sweet temptations in town. Cincinnati is home to a host of confectionary families. Here's the scoop on four of them, from the oldest to the youngest.

Graeter's

In the mid-1880s, the Graeter family came to the United States from what was known then as Bavaria. As a teenager, Louis Charles ("Charlie") Graeter worked in a market on Court Street at the foot of the Sycamore hill. One of his duties was to make ice cream. Back then, before refrigeration, he had to make it in small batches using rock salt and ice around the tub of cream and sugar to turn it into frozen ice cream. This knowledge served him well after he married Regina Berger, and they opened a store of their own. They established the first Graeter's store in 1870 in East Walnut Hills at 967 East McMillan. There they made ice cream and candies in the back of the store, sold them in the front, and lived upstairs.

Sadly, Louis Graeter's life was cut short by a streetcar accident in 1919, after which Regina not only continued to run the store but she created the phenomenal success it is now. She opened a second store in Hyde Park, which is the oldest Graeter's store still operating today.

A fourth generation of Graeters runs the company now, with stores as far away as Columbus and Lexington. In 1934, Regina bought a location on Reading Road for expanded production capability. From there, the business is run by Charlie and Regina's great-grandsons and another generation of Graeter's. CEO and president Richard Graeter says his father, Dick, who died in March 2014 at the age of 83, was the one who put their famous chocolate chips in the black raspberry ice cream. Although this became Graeter's most popular flavor, Dick claimed that he liked the plain black raspberry better.

Aglamesis Brothers

In 1908, 16-year-old Thomas Aglamesis left Sparta, Greece, and his many siblings to seek his fortune in the United States. His father had just died, and as the eldest son he needed to see to the welfare of his family. So decided to seek his fortune in the land of milk and honey. Or—more appropriately in his case—the land of butter and sugar. His brother Nicholas joined him, and they started working in downtown Cincinnati in the "Old Arcade," where they learned how to make ice cream.

When they had saved up enough to open their own place, in 1908 they bought a store in Norwood, calling it "The Metropolitan."

As the Graeters did, the Aglamesis brothers also churned all their ice cream flavors by hand, using metal cylinders with rock salt and ice to freeze the cream mixture. They soon added candies to their offerings in the store.

They bought another store in Oakley, on Madison Avenue, in 1913, where they made chocolate candy from scratch in the back. This store is the main store today and is a beauty to behold with marble counters and tabletops from Portugal, as well as Tiffany lamps. In 1922, an ice cream plant was added behind the store to expand their production. Gleaming French kettles sit in the plant in which the ice cream is made.

When the Depression hit, Thomas and Nicholas sold the Metropolitan and changed the name of their company to "Aglamesis Brothers." In the 1950s, Nicholas died and Thomas' health was failing, so Thomas' son, James, took over the company. Jim Aglamesis still runs the company today as of this writing. Another store has been added, in Montgomery. The chocolate candies and ice cream are still made in the Oakley store, the "sincere" way.

Esther Price Candies

Now wait—wasn't Esther Price from Dayton? Yes, she was. But many people in Cincinnati think she was a Cincinnatian, and the company that she founded in Dayton is now being run by a second generation of Cincinnatians, so it's worth a nod here. Esther Price was born in 1905 and died in 1994.

In a home economics class, she learned how to make fudge and her life was changed forever. Even when she graduated from school and got a job in retail, Esther continued to make candies for her friends and co-workers to great accolades.

Finally, she gave in to her destiny and opened up her own store in 1926. She prided herself on using the finest butter and cream for her candies. At one point, she asked Jim Aglamesis for advice about making candy. She created a local favorite when she and the folks

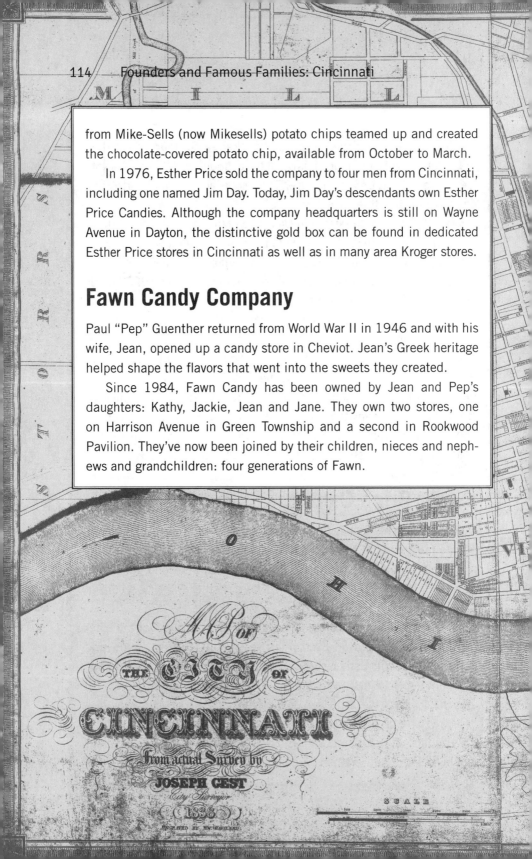

from Mike-Sells (now Mikesells) potato chips teamed up and created the chocolate-covered potato chip, available from October to March.

In 1976, Esther Price sold the company to four men from Cincinnati, including one named Jim Day. Today, Jim Day's descendants own Esther Price Candies. Although the company headquarters is still on Wayne Avenue in Dayton, the distinctive gold box can be found in dedicated Esther Price stores in Cincinnati as well as in many area Kroger stores.

Fawn Candy Company

Paul "Pep" Guenther returned from World War II in 1946 and with his wife, Jean, opened up a candy store in Cheviot. Jean's Greek heritage helped shape the flavors that went into the sweets they created.

Since 1984, Fawn Candy has been owned by Jean and Pep's daughters: Kathy, Jackie, Jean and Jane. They own two stores, one on Harrison Avenue in Green Township and a second in Rookwood Pavilion. They've now been joined by their children, nieces and nephews and grandchildren: four generations of Fawn.

∽ CHAPTER 7 ∽

START THE PRESSES!

I N THE LATE 1870S, a young man was seeking to join his family business: Edward Willis ("E. W.") Scripps, youngest of 13 children, had been forced to leave school at the age of 15 when his father's failing health forced him to take over the reins of the family farm. However, that was not the family business that he aspired to.

Other members of the Scripps family were active in the publishing world. His English grandfather, W. A. Scripps, published the London *Literary Gazette*, and his half-brother James E. Scripps was editor and president of the *Detroit Tribune*. Young Edward loved to read and write and yearned for a literary career in newspapers. He approached his half-brother James about a job, but was turned down.

In the Scripps family household in Rushville, Illinois, the blended family of 13 children from three different mothers had been rather contentious and filled with rivalries and jealousies. It is said that E. W. had not helped matters with his self-focused attitude, either.

His mother was very hard on him, frequently whipping him, deriding him, and claiming that he would surely be the one to embarrass the family. As a result, E. W.'s half-sister Ellen Browning Scripps, older by 18 years, became more like a mother to him. She maintained this role of supporter, mentor, and confidante throughout their lives.

Evidently not one to take "no" for an answer, especially not from a half-brother, E. W. made arrangements to move to Detroit under the guise of helping yet another relative open a drugstore, hoping to get a job at James's newspaper. While killing time waiting for the drugstore to open, E. W. persuaded yet another half-brother, William, who worked at the *Tribune*, to give him a job there. So at the age of 18, E. W. started as an office boy in the counting room. He never made it back to the drugstore business.

Financial losses caused James to be booted out of the *Tribune*, so on August 23, 1873, he started his own paper, the *Evening News*, and took E. W. with him. There, E. W. hit his stride.

James felt that the paper needed to be written more for the working man, so he offered it at only two cents a copy. Instead of long stories that jumped to back pages, he filled the pages with many shorter articles that kept a tired, working person's attention better. Finally, he sold his paper in the afternoon, so that a worker could pick the paper up in the afternoon on his way home and read it after dinner. It was a model that E. W. followed later in his own endeavors.

E. W. started as an apprentice in the city room, learning how to craft stories in the midst of veteran journalists. After a year he went to his brother and asked for a real job. Much to E. W.'s surprise, James agreed. He made E. W. city editor at the grand rate of $15 a week. (This was rather low even for the 1870s. James was taking advantage of his little brother; he was also notoriously frugal, instructing reporters to use both sides of a piece of paper.)

James Scripps dreamed of a newspaper empire across the country, but it was E. W. who carried it out. At 24, E. W. borrowed $10,000 from his sister Ellen to become editor of the *Cleveland Penny*

Press (which became the *Cleveland Press*). James and E. W. Scripps took over the *Penny Paper* and renamed it the *Penny Post* (which was changed to the *Cincinnati Post* in 1890).

The paper had been founded in Cincinnati in 1880 by Walter and Albert Wellman. Finally E. W. saw his chance to break free of James. They worked out an agreement whereby E. W. would move to Cincinnati and take over the *Post*, and James would move to St. Louis to take care of another newspaper they had acquired there. Finally E. W. Scripps had what he wanted: his own newspaper, an audience, and a cause: tearing down the political machine of George "Boss" Cox.

In 1889 E. W. Scripps and Milton A. McRae established the Scripps-McRae League of Newspapers. Not content with the telegraphic service provided by the Associated Press, they then created the Scripps-McRae Press Association in 1897.

E. W. Scripps wanted to ensure a free press, not a monopoly of news provided to only those who could afford to buy it. So he took his Scripps-McRae Press Association of the Midwest and the Scripps News Association on the Pacific Coast he had formed in the early 1900s and combined it with the Publishers Press, a small news service in the East that he had purchased in 1906. This new press service became the United Press Association (eventually United Press International).

As Scripps acquired more and more newspapers across the country, he spent less and less time in Cincinnati, so he launched his assaults against Boss Cox from across the country.

In 1919, E. W. Scripps had begun to pull back from management of the organization, choosing to spend most of his time on his San

Diego ranch, Miramar, and letting his sons James and Robert run his publishing empire. In 1922, the company became Scripps-Howard, reflecting the leadership of Roy Howard. (Howard had been the head of United Press and a longtime partner to E. W. Scripps.) On June 22, 1922, Scripps-Howard's motto was first used: "Give light and the people will find their own way."

Robert Scripps and Roy Howard took over the editorial and business management of the company. E. W. Scripps died on March 12, 1926, aboard his yacht *Ohio*, off the coast of Liberia, and was buried at sea. It was a strange foreshadowing of his own son's death: Robert Scripps died aboard his yacht on March 2, 1938.

E. W. Scripps's publishing empire grew far beyond his dreams into technology and venues that were unimaginable in his day. In 1935 Scripps had ventured into radio, with WCPO (which stood for the *Cincinnati Post*). In November 1939, Scripps had acquired the rights to the National Spelling Bee from the *Louisville Courier-Journal*. Shortly thereafter (1947), Scripps also launched its first television stations, which were followed eventually by shopping, gardening, do-it-yourself, and food networks. And to this day, the National Spelling Bee raises the hopes of hundreds of youngsters and their parents across the country.

In his lifetime, E. W. Scripps—with his dear sister Ellen—also endowed the Scripps Institution of Oceanography in La Jolla, California. They fully funded the Scripps Institution for the first several years. In 1912 the Scripps Institution became part of the University of California and was renamed the Scripps Institution for Biological Research, then the Scripps Institution of Oceanography in October 1925. Then in the 1960s, led by institution director Roger Revelle, the Scripps Institution of Oceanography formed the catalyst for the creation of the University of California, San Diego.

When the *Post & Times-Star* had been formed in Cincinnati by the combination of his *Post* and Charles Phelps Taft's *Times-Star*, E. W. Scripps said, "We have no politics in the sense of the word as commonly used. We are not Republican, not Democrat, not Greenback, not Prohibitionist. We simply intend to support good men and condemn bad ones, support good measures and condemn bad ones, no matter what party they belong to. We shall tell no lies about persons or policies for love, malice, or money."[1]

---

1 Dick Perry, *Vas You Ever in Zinzinnati?* (New York: Doubleday & Co., 1966), 183.

Who Runs the Cincinnati Redlegs? —from the Owners' Box

Cincinnati is appropriately proud of having the first professional baseball team. It is a team of many firsts: first time the sitting U.S. president threw out the opening day baseball (a tradition that continued for many years), first night big league game, first "wire to wire" season in 1990 under the ownership of the first woman to own a Major League Baseball team, Marge Schott. But who are the other owners to have had a piece of the Reds over the years?

1882–1890 Justus Thorner

1891–1902 John T. Bush

1902–1927 August Garry Herrman (friend of "Boss" Cox and creator of the World Series)

1927–1929 Campbell Johnson ("C.J.") McDiarmid

1929–1933 Sidney Weil

1934–1961 Powel Crosley, Jr.

1961–1966 Bill DeWitt (whose son owned the Cardinals)

1967–1973 Francis L. Dale (with Bill DeWitt, Jr.) (publisher of the *Cincinnati Enquirer*)

1973–1980 Louis Nippert

1980–1984 William and James Williams (minority owners over a group that included Marge Schott)

1984–1999 Marge Schott

1999–2005 Carl H. Lindner, Jr. (over a group, but Schott remained in the minority)

2005–present Robert Castellini (over a group that included Lindner until the time of his death in 2011)

And just what *is* the name of the team? Well, from 1882 to 1889, they were the Cincinnati Red Stockings. Then from 1890 to 1953, they were the Cincinnati Reds. However, from 1954 to 1959, they were the Cincinnati Redlegs before going back to being our Cincinnati Reds—which they remain today.

~ CHAPTER 8 ~

TRAILBLAZERS

I N 1854, Rabbi Isaac Wise arrived in Cincinnati with his wife, Therese, from Albany, New York, where he had already begun implementing a series of changes in how Jews practiced their faith. He had dropped the bar mitzvah in favor of confirmation, instituted choral singing, and integrated the seating of men and women in the service. (These changes were not welcomed by all. He had been dismissed from his former post in 1850.)

Wise had already begun to gain a national reputation, so it is not surprising that he was invited by the Cincinnati congregation of B'nai Yeshurun to preach a guest sermon. However, what is surprising is that he said he would come if they named him their permanent pastor, sight unseen. They did, so he came. He continued his reforms upon his arrival in Cincinnati and being elected rabbi by B'nai Yeshurun.

Soon he became known as the founder of American Reform Judaism. At the same time, the more orthodox B'nai Israel was without a leader. Although they were orthodox, they also asked Rabbi Wise to lead them—which he did for a year, until replaced by his friend Rabbi Max Lilienthal.

The B'nai Yeshurun congregation at this time was about 20 years old and consisted of about 200 families. When they decided it was time to build a temple, however, they solicited Rabbi Wise's input. He saw this congregation and this city as being the beginning of the home of the next Golden Age of Jewish Life. He had the Plum Street Temple built to hold more than a thousand people.

Dr. Isaac Wise made Cincinnati his home for the rest of his life, establishing the *Israelite* newspaper here (which became the *American Israelite* in 1874 and is still published in Cincinnati today).

In 1855, Rabbis Wise and Lilienthal founded Zion College, which then became Hebrew Union College 20 years later, the first Jewish theological seminary in the United States. With the leadership of Isaac Mayer Wise and Max Lilienthal, Cincinnati became the home of American Reform Judaism.

Wise was the father to many. In addition to being the father of American Reform Judaism, Dr. Wise was also literally the father to 10 children. One daughter, Effie, married Adolph Ochs, from an old Cincinnati Jewish family. Adolph was the eldest of three

sons. The younger two sons, George and Milton, became journalists in Pennsylvania and Tennessee. Adolph, with Effie at his side, overhauled the *Chattanooga Times*, then rescued and resurrected the *New York Times* in 1896.

One Cincinnati humanitarian who had national impact but was not well known by name was Irvin Ferdinand

Westheimer. One day in July 1903, he prepared to enter his building where he ran a sales office for his father's business, the Westheimer Distillery. He noticed a small boy digging through the trash cans with his dog. Approaching the young boy, he introduced himself. He learned the boy, named Tom (the dog's name was "Gyp"), didn't have a father but had four siblings and a very hard-working mother. Westheimer took the boy to a restaurant for some food. The next week he took him to see a Reds game. They developed a friendship over time; Tom began calling Irvin his "big brother."

Because of that one friendship, Westheimer then asked his friends and associates to look out for boys in similar situations. This idea grew into a national movement that eventually became the Big Brothers of America. In 1908, Mrs. Cornelius Vanderbilt began a similar organization, which became the Big Sisters of America. (The two joined, forming Big Brothers Big Sisters of America in 1979.)

Another Cincinnati son, Robert Irvin Westheimer, son of Irvin F. Westheimer, was about to follow in his father's philanthropic footsteps. After graduating from Walnut Hills High School, he went to Cornell University in Ithaca, New York, but he returned to Cincinnati after graduating in 1938. Like many of Cincinnati's founding family members, he saw the world and touched the world, but returned home to do his greatest works.

Robert Westheimer married Ruth E. Welling on November 12, 1945, and thus began a "partnership of social service," as their son, Richard, described it later. Like his father, Irvin, Robert Westheimer dedicated his life to helping the community at large, and specifically the young and the poor through such organizations as the Boys & Girls Clubs, the Greater Cincinnati Foundation, United Appeal and his father's own Big Brothers Big Sisters. In business, he retired as the director emeritus of Cincinnati Financial Corporation and served on the boards of many organizations.

Besides son Richard, Ruth and Robert Westheimer also had two daughters: Ann and Sallie. Like her grandfather Irvin Westheimer,

Sallie dedicated much of her life to helping the community's children, helping to found an organization to help parents identify child care to fit their needs. Comprehensive Community Child Care (now called 4C for Children) was established in 1972 to help train child care personnel. It has since expanded and has made Greater Cincinnati a national model in the availability and quality of child care.

On November 25, 1903, William DeHart Hubbard was born, the eldest of what would ultimately be William and Carrie Hubbard's eight children. "DeHart" grew up fast and strong, attending Douglass School and then Walnut Hills High School, where he excelled both academically and athletically. Looking at him through the lens of the twenty-first century, he clearly had a good future waiting for him in college. But back then, with opportunities for African Americans limited, where would that future be?

DeHart Hubbard had caught the attention of University of Michigan alumnus Lon Barringer. Barringer, a resident of West Virginia, had followed the high school career of young DeHart in the Cincinnati newspapers and felt the young man's strong athletic and academic prowess that he exhibited while at Walnut Hills High School would be a good fit at University of Michigan. He knew that head football coach and fellow West Virginian Fielding Yost had prohibited other African Americans from playing for Michigan. However, he also knew that Yost had just been named Michigan's athletic director.

Fortunately for Michigan and Hubbard, the *Cincinnati Enquirer* was holding a contest to increase their subscription base with the intent to help local high school students. The students who brought in the most new subscriptions would win a full-ride $3,000 scholarship to the college of their choice. In a very unorthodox move, Barringer convinced DeHart to enter the contest with the promise that he would do everything he could to help him. Barringer sent a letter to almost every Michigan alum in the country, as well as DeHart's

Cincinnati supporters. As a result, William DeHart Hubbard was able to enroll at the University of Michigan in September 1921.

DeHart excelled at Michigan, participating in track and field. As a freshman, he was unable to participate in varsity events, but he was able to participate in an AAU event in New Jersey. His success at that event qualified him for the 1924 Paris Olympics (the setting for the movie *Chariots of Fire*). As an African American, he was not allowed to participate in all the events for which he qualified, but he was allowed to do the running long jump—and jump he did! He won the gold medal, the first African American from the United States to win an Olympic gold medal in an individual event: 12 years before Jesse Owens. He competed again in the 1928 Olympics.

Hubbard returned to America and to the University of Michigan, where the following year he set a world record for the long jump (25 feet, 10¾ inches). In 1926 he then tied the world record for the 100-yard dash (9.6 seconds). DeHart Hubbard graduated from the University of Michigan in 1927 with honors, and as a three-time track-and-field NCAA All American and seven-time track-and-field Big Ten Conference champion.

"Negro boy near Cincinnati, Ohio," photo by John Vachon (1914–1975), taken circa 1942 or 1943 for the Farm Security Administration

Credit: Library of Congress

Upon graduation he went to work for the Cincinnati Public Recreation Commission to encourage recreation and organize community events. He started by surveying the recreational facilities available to African Americans, similar to a study done in 1913. Not surprisingly, he found limited activities for both children and adults.

After Cincinnati hosted the annual National Conference of Colored Recreation Workers in 1932, Hubbard asked National Recreation Association representative Ernest Ten Eyck Attwell to stay behind to conduct a survey of the needs of the African American community.

One of Attwell's findings was that there was no musical/cultural outlet for the African American community for "mass expression in a musical way." He noted this as a major deficiency in the recreation program.

There was no Black Family Reunion or Juneteenth Celebration, for example, as Cincinnatians enjoy today. At that time, African Americans were not even allowed in the May Festival Chorus. So in June of 1938, a loosely formed June Festival Chorus was established, with Paul Robeson performing many times as soloist. In some years, the chorus did not perform, but historical records don't indicate the reason.

Perhaps because of the rising suspicion of Robeson and his alleged Communistic allegiance, eventually the Recreation Commission withdrew its support of the June Festival Chorus. The chorus did last for 20 years, however. The May Festival Chorus also became integrated during this time.

Scientist, philanthropist, and former May Festival Chorus member Ernest L. Robinson with Joyce van Wye at *La Bohème* reception at CCM.

Credit: University of Cincinnati Photo Services

In 1956, May Festival's first African-American soloists, Leontyne Price and William Warfield, performed excerpts from "Porgy and Bess" and starred in the world premiere choral performance of "Spoon River" by composer Wallace Berry.

Hubbard eventually moved to Cleveland where he worked for the Federal Public Housing Authority. His athletic abilities and commitment to public service were later reflected in his great-nephew, one-time football player at Xavier University, Cincinnati mayor, and Ohio Secretary of State, J. Kenneth Blackwell.

As a very young child, Loretta Catherine Cessor began playing the piano in her hometown of Gallipolis, in southeastern Ohio, just across the Ohio River from West Virginia. It was a sign of things to come. Loretta played for her church as a teenager and then moved on to helping support the family with earnings from playing for parties.

She moved to Cincinnati with her husband, William Langston Manggrum, in 1926, where Loretta continued to earn money from her playing by working at theatres, playing the music during the silent movies. At this point she also began to try her hand at composition. She continued to teach, compose, and perform while raising four children. William Manggrum, who had earned his pharmacy degree on June 15, 1921, from the University of Pittsburgh, opened a drug store at Park and Chapel Streets in the Walnut Hills neighborhood in the 1920s, where he often trained other pharmacists, until he closed the store in 1953.

Loretta Manggrum became the first African American to matriculate and receive a degree from the Conservatory of Music (later to become UC's College-Conservatory of Music). After earning her diploma from Hughes High School at the age of 49, she earned a bachelor of music degree from the Ohio State University in 1951. She earned her master's degree in 1953 when she was 57.

After her children were grown, Loretta taught in the Cincinnati Public School System for 10 years at Garfield Elementary School. When she retired, she began work on her doctorate and served as choir director and organist at Gaines United Methodist Church in the Madisonville neighborhood of Cincinnati. She donated her works to the Library of Congress and then went on to receive an honorary doctorate in music composition and theory from UC in 1985 at the age of 88.

Another Cincinnatian started out in Gallipolis: Marian Alexander. She, along with her brothers and twin sister, Mildred, often struggled in the segregated town, fighting for the right to attend high school with white children, for example, and fighting to be allowed into the National Honor Society. Marian joined the NAACP at the

Marian Spencer's smile lit up the Shoemaker Center for UC's Fall 2006 Commencement, December 9, 2006. Both Spencers received honorary doctorates of humane letters.

Credit: Dottie Stover/University of Cincinnati Photo Services

age of 13. Marian and Mildred were co-valedictorians of their high school class.

Marian and Mildred Alexander came to Cincinnati from their hometown after high school to study at the University of Cincinnati. Because African Americans were not allowed in the residence halls, the Alexander twins lived with the Manggrums. (Loretta Manggrum was their father's cousin.) They worked in their cousin Bill's drugstore for one whole day. That was the extent of their employment at the Manggrum Drug Store, for Bill Manggrum said that they smiled at the customers too much. Anyone who has ever met Marian Alexander Spencer will find this easy to believe, for she was the young woman who was considered too cheerful for pharmaceutical work.

Marian's future husband, Donald Spencer, had already graduated from college and was teaching at the Douglass School when he met Marian and Mildred Alexander. While still an education major, Donald had formed an organization called Quadres to unite people of all races and to end racial discrimination at the university. At the time, African Americans were constrained as to what colleges they were allowed in (Teachers College and Liberal Arts, for the most part), and they were not allowed to fully participate in all activities in and around campus, such as acting in the school theatre productions or swimming in the YMCA pool. Not one to be dissuaded, Donald had Quadres put on its own musicals to raise money for their activities, acting in many of the productions himself. Marian had found a kindred spirit.

Donald was the first African American to become a licensed Realtor in Cincinnati. He and Marian were married on August 28, 1940, while Marian was still a UC student. She and her sister graduated in 1942.

Besides having a smile that would light up a room (not just Manggrum's drug store), Marian Spencer had spunk, too. In the early 1950s, Spencer heard the many radio advertisements that Coney Island welcoming all children in Cincinnati. When she called the amusement park to ask about the ads, she told them that she was an African American. She was then told that no, actually the ad was directed at all the white children in Cincinnati. Spencer (among others) sued Coney Island in 1952 to open its doors to African Americans. Still the park resisted. The city finally announced in 1955 that it might not renew Coney Island's license if it did not allow in African Americans, so the park relented. However, Sunlite Pool—the largest recirculating swimming pool in North America—was still restricted to whites only. Not until May 1961 was it opened to all people, regardless of color or ethnicity.

Founding Fathers

Transplants to Cincinnati often experience a similar phenomenon in a simple question: "Where did you go to school?"

"Virginia Tech," I answered, when I was first asked.

"No, high school," was usually the reply. In the beginning, I was perplexed. Why would anyone in Ohio care where I went to high school?

"Monument Mountain Regional High School," I would say each time. "In Great Barrington, Massachusetts."

"Oh, you're not from around here," was the usual response.

I soon learned that Cincinnatians care very deeply about many things and right at the top of that list was where people went to high school. Some say this caring is a matter of judgment, but it's more likely a matter of camaraderie.

Cincinnatians feel a strong bond with their schools: especially the Roman Catholic institutions. And there are a lot of them. If you're talking grade schools, you can't spit without hitting a Catholic elementary school.

As far as the high schools go, the Cincinnati Archdiocese has many high schools, of which 14 are in Cincinnati proper. Four are all male; five are all female; and five are co-ed. The names of these schools conjure up strong feelings of allegiance in some and bitter rivalries in others: St. Xavier, Moeller, Elder, Ursuline, Mount Notre Dame, and Mother of Mercy—just to name a few.

But before some names proudly adorned the façade of institutes of learning, they were the humble names of leaders in the Cincinnati community. Here's a sample.

Purcell: Of the accomplishments under Archbishop John Baptist Purcell's tenure, two stand out in particular. Pope Pius IX elevated Cincinnati to an Archdiocese on July 19, 1850. St. Peter in Chains was designated the Cathedral of the Archdiocese in 1851 (with a brief break during which St. Monica in University Heights assumed the title). The Sycamore Street church (the original location of St. Peter in Chains) and Athenaeum (the school) were then passed to the

Jesuits. In 1860, the Jesuits created St. Xavier College, comprising a high school and a college. The school grew. Xavier University moved to Victory Parkway in 1919 and St. Xavier High School moved to North Bend Road in 1960. What remains today at the Sycamore Street site is St. Francis Xavier church and a parking lot.

Archbishop Purcell fervently felt that the Bible should be read by all school children, however, he feared that the Protestant King James Version of the Bible that was being used in the public schools was inappropriate for Catholic children. In fact, the Ohio constitution of 1851 read, in part, that "no religious sect or other sects shall ever have any exclusive right to, or control of, any part of the school funds of this state." Purcell felt that reading of the Protestant Bible and singing Protestant hymns was in violation of this constitution. At one point, Archbishop Purcell decreed that Catholic children should attend only Catholic schools. Finally he formally protested, in a battle that went as high as the Ohio Supreme Court.

What is now called Purcell Marian High School is in the neighborhood of East Walnut Hills off of Madison Road. Archbishop Henry Moeller originally planned to build the school for the St. Francis de Sales parish where Walnut Hills High School is now. However, after Moeller's death in 1925, Archbishop John Timothy McNicholas decided to move the location of the school to Hackberry Street, where it is now, and to name the school for former Archbishop Purcell, who had died in 1883. The school was completed in 1928 and served as an all-boys' Catholic high school. Meanwhile, St. Mary's school in Hyde Park, built in 1908, had been a coeducational parish elementary and secondary school. When Purcell High School was completed, the boys were transferred there and an all-girl diocesan high school named "St. Mary's" was designated in 1928. In 1963, St. Mary's became Marian High School (this building is now Springer School). In 1980, Purcell and Marian merged, graduating their first co-ed class in 1985.

Elder: William Henry Elder was the second archbishop of Cincinnati. Born in Maryland in 1819, he received a doctorate of divinity in Rome where he was also ordained in 1846. He was appointed to be Bishop of Natchez (Mississippi), where he first showed his mettle. During

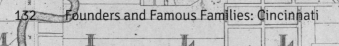

the Civil War, he was ordered by the Federal troops there to have the churches in his parish say prayers publicly for the president of the United States. He refused. He was tried, convicted, and briefly served jail time in Louisiana until the ruling was overturned in Washington, D.C. After a lengthy term as the Bishop of Natchez, he was then appointed the Archbishop of Cincinnati, serving from 1883 to 1904.

While archbishop, Elder reopened the theological seminary (Mt. St. Mary, on Beechmont Avenue), founded St. Gregory's Preparatory Seminary, and enlarged St. Joseph's Orphan Asylum. He revived the failing coffers from Archbishop Purcell's tenure, demanding that priests and parishes submit regular financial statements to the archdiocese. He died from influenza in 1904.

Ground was broken for Elder High School in 1922. It originally educated both male and female high school students, but when St. Vincent Academy reopened its doors in 1927 as all-girl Seton High School two blocks away, Elder High School became an all-boys' high school.

Moeller: At Archbishop Elder's request, Archbishop Henry K. Moeller (born December 11, 1849) was named coadjutor for Archbishop Elder, because of the archbishop's advancing years and failing health. Dr. Moeller (having received his Doctor of Divinity from Pontifical Urban College in Rome in 1876) had been a priest in Cincinnati but at the time was serving as Bishop of Columbus. Elder's petition was granted April 27, 1903. Moeller was installed as Chancellor of the archdiocese in June 1903. Elder turned over most of the administrative duties of the archdiocese to his coadjutor, even adding a codicil to his will, making Moeller his sole heir.

Under his leadership as the fourth Archbishop of Cincinnati, Archbishop Henry Moeller oversaw the rapidly growing Cincinnati archdiocese. Since 1904, 28 new parishes had been formed and new religious communities had been formed, such as the Sisters of St. Ursula on McMillan St. (now also the site of St. Ursula Academy), the Dominican Nuns of St. Catherine de Ricci, and the Second Order of St. Dominic. The Fenwick Club was established, the Bureau of

Catholic Charities was created, a new theological seminary building was erected in Norwood, and the Apostolic Mission Band was created.

Archbishop Moeller might be best known for establishing the arch-diocesan school system and the court battles around those efforts. Moeller, like Elder before him, believed that children should have access to a free education provided by the state. However, in 1915, when the city started providing Protestant Bibles to the schools and requiring that all children read them, Moeller objected. The Protestant Bible differs from the Catholic Bible (See Chapter 2, Law and Order). Still wanting students to have access to a free education, one of Moeller's achievements was the creation of two "mega" high schools, established through pooling the resources of multiple parishes, where students could obtain a Catholic education free of charge. And thus Elder was built on the west side and Purcell was built on the east. After more than 20 years of leadership, Archbishop Moeller died on January 5, 1925. To honor his service, Archbishop Moeller High School was established, serving the northeastern side of Cincinnati since 1960.

McNicholas: John Timothy McNicholas had the strange distinction of having been given two appointments in the same year. He was named Bishop of the Indianapolis Diocese in May 1925 and the Archbishop of Cincinnati's Archdiocese in July 1925. (The Indianapolis appoint-ment did not take effect.) Of McNicholas's 48½ years as a man of the cloth, 31½ of them were as a bishop.

He had been born Timothy McNicholas in Ireland in 1877 and emigrated from Ireland with his parents when he was 4. He ended up in Kentucky and Ohio, was educated in Catholic schools, and was ordained at the age of 24 by Bishop Henry Moeller in 1901, taking "John" as his religious name. He continued his studies, earning a doctorate in sacred theology in Rome. McNicholas served and stud-ied abroad and in New York City and Duluth, Minnesota, where he was appointed Bishop of Duluth. His curious "dual appointment" year of 1925 arose when he was appointed the Bishop of Indianapolis at the same time that Joseph Chartrand was named Archbishop of Cincinnati. Chartrand refused the appointment. So McNicholas was installed as Archbishop of Cincinnati, and Chartrand was installed as Bishop of Indianapolis.

McNicholas served in that capacity for the rest of his life—25 years. Throughout his service and studies, he was known for embracing people of other cultures. He vehemently denounced Hitler's treatment of the Jewish people during the Holocaust. He was also known for his crusades against what he termed immoral movies, forming the "Catholic Legion of Decency" (CLOD). He was joined in his fight by Protestants and Jews, and the group became known as the National Legion of Decency.

In 1950 he directed that St. Mary High School, on the eastern edge of the city, should be designated the first coeducational Catholic high school. He died suddenly of a heart attack in his College Hill home at the age of 72. His successor, Archbishop Karl Alter, had the school name changed to Archbishop McNicholas High School in his honor.

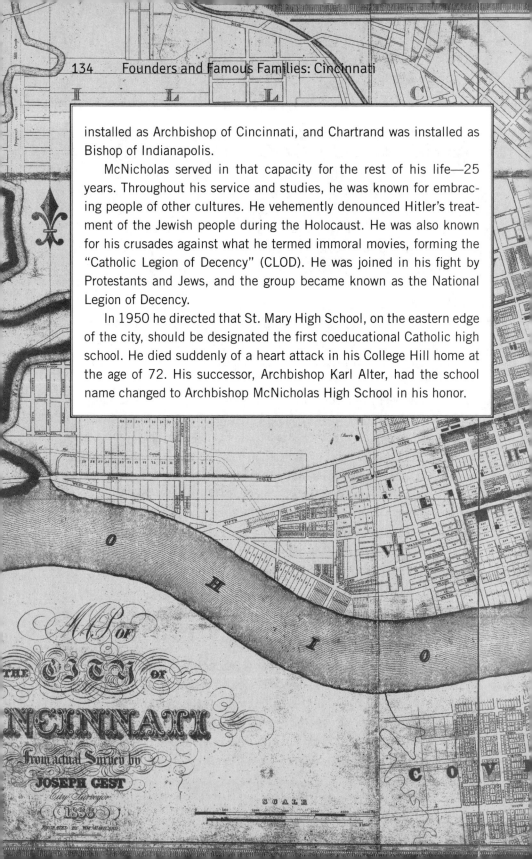

~ CHAPTER 9 ~

LEADING LADIES

N 1868, Maria Longworth married Civil War veteran Col. George Nichols. This marriage between two of Cincinnati's founding families resulted in one of the Western Hemisphere's longest-standing traditions. In 1872, Col. and Mrs. Nichols were entertaining the German conductor Theodore Thomas at their home, when Mrs. Nichols showed Thomas a program from the Birmingham Music Festival in England. She asked why something similar could not be done in Cincinnati. Thomas's response was positive. Both Nicholses immediately jumped on the idea and put plans in motion for a Cincinnati music festival for the following spring.

A planning committee formed, composed of men with such familiar names as Col. George Nichols, John Shillito, and Bellamy Storer Jr., as well as many musicians and members of the Harmonic Society. The plan was to hold the concert in the Exhibition Hall.

The debut performances in May 1873 were tremendous and received national acclaim. A subsequent concert was planned for 1875.

Again, community leaders participated on the planning committee. Theodore Thomas planned to be at the podium. All was ready for the opening of *Lohengrin*. Just as the opening notes were to be played, however, the heavens opened and a deluge of raindrops hit the metal roof of Exhibition Hall. Thomas signaled for the orchestra to stop. He turned to the audience and asked if he should continue. Finally the rain eased and the concert could go on.

One person in the audience that night resolved never to go through that again. Reuben Springer proposed that he would put up $125,000—which he estimated was half of the cost of a new musical auditorium—if the other half could be raised by the community. Thus began a major push, including schoolchildren saving pennies, to build Music Hall, which is the home of the Cincinnati May Festival to this day. Bounding Music Hall on the east side was Elm Street and the Miami & Erie Canal on the west. Across the canal was the Insane Asylum, right where Cincinnati Public Radio now stands.

Music Hall was designed by Samuel Hannaford, Cincinnati's premier architect. Although his work can be seen in New England, the South, and throughout the Midwest, most of Hannaford's work is in the Greater Cincinnati area. He also designed Cincinnati's City Hall (with his sons Harvey and

Samuel Hannaford built Cincinnati's City Hall, which stands to the right of St. Peter in Chains Cathedral.

Credit: Historic American Buildings Survey, Library of Congress.

Charles), old St. George Church (on Calhoun Street), and the Workhouse (which was demolished in 1991).

Maria Longworth is credited with being the first woman to play such an important role in founding a musical festival, the Cincinnati May Festival, and in the construction of Music Hall itself. However, she is better known in Cincinnati for being the first woman to have her own manufacturing business: Rookwood Pottery, named for her grandfather's estate.

Maria Longworth had long been enamored with art and the craft of painting pottery. It is said that Maria Longworth Nichols had been miffed when she did not receive an invitation to join a ladies' pottery club in Cincinnati. The club assured her they had sent the invitation; she just hadn't received it. Indignant still, Ms. Longworth started her own group. In 1876 she had her work exhibited at Philadelphia's Centennial Exposition. In 1879 she commissioned the building of a special kind of pottery kiln for the type of painting she was doing. Her father, Joseph, purchased an old barn, which he turned into a studio for her creations and thus Rookwood Pottery was born in 1880.

Back when Joseph's mother, Susan Howell Conner Longworth, died, the family had decided that they no longer needed the sprawling Belmont Estate on Pike Street, in downtown Cincinnati. They sold it in 1866 for $100,000 to a druggist named F. E. Suire. Unfortunately, his pharmacy failed and in 1873 Belmont was sold to Irishman David Sinton.

Sinton was a self-made man of the truest kind, working hard and pinching pennies until he became one of the chief financiers of Cincinnati Gas & Electric as well as Cleveland Gas. His only child, Anna, shared his frugality. She soon caught the eye of Charles Phelps Taft, son of Judge Alphonso Taft, and she married him in 1873 in her father's home—the Belmont, the former Baum-Longworth estate.

The newlyweds moved in with Mr. Sinton, as he was a widower by then. Anna Sinton Taft discovered that at some point pharmacist

Suire had wallpapered over eight mural landscape panels in the main hall of the mansion, which were attributed to Robert S. Duncanson, an African American artist of the antebellum period whom Nicholas Longworth had sponsored.

Duncanson was a descendant of Virginia freed slaves. In 1842 he had had his first exhibition in Cincinnati, but his family was not allowed to attend because they were African American. Duncanson continued to paint and studied to perfect his art, but with the Civil War threatening, Duncanson exiled himself to Canada and the United Kingdom.

Charles Phelps Taft, who had been a congressman and at one time owned the Chicago Cubs, died on December 31, 1929. In 1930, his widow, Anna Sinton Taft ("Annie") donated $5 million to the University of Cincinnati and endowed a research fund in her husband's memory. Today known as the Charles Phelps Taft Research Center in the McMicken College of Arts & Sciences, it supports undergraduate, graduate, and faculty research across 13 departments. The center's mission is to "promote scholarly research through fellowships and awards; foster critical conversations across disciplines; create and sustain an intellectual community for the exchange of ideas; and support lectures, conferences, seminars, study groups, and symposia in the Taft disciplines." Taft descendants still manage the family endowment.

Joseph Longworth strongly supported the arts in Cincinnati, both specifically through his commitment to his daughter, Maria, and to the arts in general. When merchandiser Charles West offered $150,000 toward building a new art museum if matching funds could be raised, Joseph Longworth pledged $37,000. Part of the arrangement was that the art museum would be separated from the University of Cincinnati. The Cincinnati Art Museum was thus built in Eden Park, which had been originally part of the Nicholas Longworth estate, with the School of Design established as a separate Art Academy endowed by Joseph and Nicholas Longworth II,

David Sinton, Reuben Springer, and M. E. Ingalls. Covington's Frank Duveneck dedicated the last 25 years of his life at the Museum and left 40 of his paintings to the Cincinnati Art Museum at his death.

Meanwhile, Maria Longworth Nichols's Rookwood Pottery was experiencing great success. Despite her fantastic professional accomplishments, however, she was not experiencing complete happiness at home. When she married Col. George Nichols, her father had given them a portion of the Longworth Rookwood property for their home.

Unfortunately, as marital frictions continued to arise between the high-spirited Colonel and Mrs. Nichols, they prepared to divorce. Maria—who by this time had fallen in love with Bellamy Storer and who owned the Nicholses' house—had an identical house constructed 25 feet away from their home, with the two connected by underground tunnel and a walkway between the second stories. It was her intent that she would neither boot her soon-to-be-ex-husband out into the cold nor force their children to go to any hardship to see their father. This way, the children could see either parent any time they wished. The unusual plan was that Maria and Bellamy Storer would move into the new house in 1886. However, all her plans were unnecessary, as George Nichols died in 1885. At Col. Nichols's death, Storer simply married Maria Longworth Nichols and moved into the old house.

Bellamy Storer had been a friend of both Nicholses before marrying Maria and had been active in many of the same causes, such as establishing the Cincinnati May Festival and building Music Hall. After the marriage, the Storers became very active in Washington politics and were closely allied with both President William McKinley and Teddy Roosevelt. Unfortunately, they also became very active in religious politics, too.

By the 1880s, in addition to Thomas Emery's lard oil factory, the property management side of their father's business was flourishing under the Emery sons' hands. Thomas Emery's Sons, Incorporated (which became Emery Industries, Inc., in 1928, and was much later merged into National Distillers) built hotels, apartment houses, and business buildings all over Cincinnati. Tom, the older brother, felt that some of the other hotels in town were profiting too much off their guests and offered rates about 50 percent below those of the best hotels, such as the Burnet and the Grand. The Emerys built the Palace Hotel in 1882 and charged two dollars a day for room and board.

Thomas J. Emery married Mary Hopkins in 1866; Samuel Hannaford built their family home, the Edgecliffe, which over-looked the Ohio River. However, theirs was not to remain a happy family for long. They had two sons: Sheldon, born in 1867, and Albert, born in 1868. Albert died at the age of 16 as the result of a sledding accident, and Sheldon died at 23 from pneumonia while a student at Harvard. Thomas died in 1906, leaving his widow a lonely millionaire for 21 years. He left her his $20 million fortune with no directives as to how to spend it.

However, Mary Emery (known as "Guppy" to her friends) saw that she had what she called a "vast responsibility" to the people of Cincinnati and opened her purse and her heart to them. She became known as "Lady Bountiful" as she stepped in like an angel and saved the opera, the zoo, Holmes Hospital, and many other organizations that were on the cusp of nonexistence. She donated an entire wing and more than $3 million worth of art from her own collection to the Cincinnati Art Museum.

Her largest gesture of largesse is probably Mariemont (pro-nounced MARE-ee-mont), arguably one of the first planned com-munities in the United States. She felt that the living conditions in downtown Cincinnati were deplorable, so she procured a large tract of land on the east side of town. Working with architect John Nolen, she endeavored to create a community with an English country gar-den feel. They named it Mariemont, after her estate in Rhode Island, which her beloved Thomas had built for her.

Mary Emery died in 1927 at the age of 83. Tom and Mary Emery had no heirs; younger brother John was still a bachelor in his 60s, so he married a 22-year-old woman and had five children to pass on the family name and philanthropic tradition. That tradition was carried on in John J. Emery Jr., who also enjoyed success in the hotel business, building the 48-story Carew Tower (Cincinnati's tallest building at the time), the Netherland Plaza, and the Terrace Plaza hotels. He also founded Cincinnati Country Day School and held leadership roles with the Boy Scouts of America and the Cincinnati Art Museum. Meanwhile, his sister Audrey showed herself for having a flair for fashion and flings. She was voted one of the ten most beautiful women in America and married into Russian nobility not once, but twice, including the Grand Duke Dmitri Pavlovich, the cousin of Nicholas, Russia's last czar.

A Rose by Any Other Name

Henry Wadsworth Longfellow, in his poem "Catawba Wine," wasn't the first person to refer to Cincinnati as the "Queen of the West." Residents had been referring to Cincinnati as the Queen City for decades before that. On May 4, 1819, Edward B. Cooke wrote in the weekly *Inquisitor Cincinnati Advertiser,* "The City is, indeed, justly styled the fair Queen of the West: distinguished for order, enterprise, public spirit, and liberality, she stands the wonder of an admiring world."

It was one of Cooke's last editorials as the paper was restructured the following week with Cooke's two fellow co-publishers producing the paper without him. (In 1841, John and Charles Brough bought the *Advertiser* and changed its name to the *Enquirer.*)

Besides being known as the Queen City by the early 1800s, Cincinnati had another nickname that developed about the same time: Porkopolis. Evidence exists from as early as 1809 bearing witness to the regulation of pork packing for use other than personal consumption. Cincinnati had clearly earned the nickname of Porkopolis for its meat processing and products, for by this time it was the number one producer of hog products in the nation.

Both hogs (slower, more domesticated fatbacks) and razorbacks (larger, fiercer, and more boar-like animals) were brought en masse through Cincinnati proper. The town's access to the Ohio River proved to be a boon to the meat market, preventing the animals from losing as much as 200 pounds or a fifth of their body weight while being driven to the killing pens.

By the 1820s, the moniker of Porkopolis had been documented in the letters of bank president George W. Jones to his bank's correspondent in Liverpool. Many tales were told about Cincinnati's hog herds roaming the streets (at times being overcome by the heat until refreshed by fire hoses) while on their way to market. Sadly for these little piggies, though, when they went to market they didn't come back, unlike the fate of the piggies in the children's rhyme.

Cincinnati held the title of top pork producer until the Civil War, when losing access to the Mississippi River hurt Cincinnati's shipping capabilities. Chicago, with its superior railroads, usurped Cincinnati's position as top hog. But in its heyday of the 1830s and '40s, Cincinnati was processing more than 85,000 hogs a year in more than 25 processing plants.

The most tenacious nicknames seem to be those that arise spontaneously, by grassroots groundswell. Nicknames that are intentionally created (often by marketers and public relations experts) are well thought out, but lack the spontaneity and sense of misbehaving. In the 1980s, the Greater Cincinnati Chamber of Commerce attempted to change Cincinnati's nickname to attract companies to the city to invest, move, and hire local workers. Hence, the "Queen City" was recrowned the "Blue Chip City." It didn't stick.

The most recent effort has been in the 21st century, taking advantage of Cincinnati's great musical heritage, its May Festival, and its wonderful "One City, One Symphony" program with the Cincinnati Symphony. Spurred on by the late Erich Kunzel, director emeritus of the Cincinnati Pops, Cincinnati hosted the World Choir Games in 2012. So in 2012, Cincinnati became "The City That Sings." It's already been pretty quiet lately.

Long live the Queen!

CHAPTER 10

MUSIC TO OUR EARS

AFTER THE FIRST WORLD WAR, Cincinnati's Symphony was struggling financially. Mr. and Mrs. Charles P. Taft (the elders) stepped forward with a vision for an Institute of Fine Arts that would take care of the orchestra, assist the local schools in providing music, art, and drama to the children, and establish their own home as an art museum. They pledged $1 million toward this goal if others would contribute an additional $2.5 million.

Mrs. Charles Phelps Taft was one of two powerful women in Cincinnati who were key in seeing that that the arts thrived in Cincinnati. For many years, the arts in Cincinnati enjoyed the patronage of Anna Sinton Taft and Mrs. Mary Emery. In 1927, C. P. Taft—at the time the treasurer of the May Festival Association—and his wife came up with an idea for an ongoing organization that would be dedicated to supporting the arts in Cincinnati, instead of having families stepping in as angels or saviors when the various arts organizations needed to be rescued financially. Thus the Institute of Fine Arts was born. The Tafts offered their mansion on Fourth Street, as well as an additional $1 million, and challenged other founding families to donate as well. An additional $2.7 million was raised from these other families and the community.

The Tafts ended up giving another $1 million, thus marking the beginning of the Fine Arts Fund, an annual campaign in support of four local arts organizations: the Cincinnati Art Museum, the Cincinnati Opera, the Cincinnati Symphony Orchestra, and the Taft Museum. In 1978, the fund was expanded to include support for the Cincinnati Ballet, the Contemporary Arts Center, the Cincinnati Playhouse in the Park, and the May Festival. In addition, a projects pool was added to provide smaller, one-time grants to arts organizations in the region. In 2010, the Fine Arts Fund became "ArtsWave," to represent the ripple effect throughout the community of supporting the arts.

Things were not completely rosy in the early 1900s. With many taverns closing because of Prohibition, Cincinnatians looked for other sources of entertainment (just as many people did around the country). Radio was in its infancy in those days. Few people had radios in their homes, as the Cincinnati-made crystal sets cost more than $120 each: more than 10 times a week's wages. Even more scarce were radio broadcasts (to use the term lightly). One source about 10 miles away could be picked up.

Toward the end of the 1880s, a lawyer and his wife welcomed the first of their two children into their family, a son. Their son would grow up to refer to himself as holding "50 jobs in 50 years." Named for his father, Powel Crosley Jr. became an entrepreneur extraordinaire known both locally and nationally for his inventions and his manufacturing and business acumen.

Powel Crosley Jr. had a young son named Powel, also. Nine-year-old Powel III wanted a radio and begged his father for one. Rather than spend the unreasonable amount for a crystal set, and being an enterprising man, Crosley went to a store and bought $25 worth of parts, including a condenser, headphones, a tuning coil, and a crystal detector. He also bought a 25-cent booklet called *The A. B. C. of Radio* by Waldemar Bernhard Kaempffert. With this he built a functioning radio set for his son.

Crosley then challenged himself: he felt that he could mass-produce radio sets even more cheaply, especially if he built them without a crystal. With the assistance of two engineering students from the University of Cincinnati and his brother Lewis, he began manufacturing radios for the retail price of $20 each. Besides removing the crystal, another cost-saving move was making the cabinet for the radio out of a fairly new material: plastic. His goal, he said, was to "make available to the average man, at prices he could pay, the luxuries which, heretofore, only the rich man could afford."

Crosley called the radio a "Harko," as in the word "hark," meaning "to listen." He ended up expanding his manufacturing operations four times, making as many as 500 sets a day, and underpricing his competitors.

At the same time that he was creating an empire in radio set construction, he also tackled the other side of the radio set: the radio airwaves. Powel Crosley Jr. began to broadcast. In July 1921 he started by playing his own collection of LPs from his home under the call signal of 8CR with all the power of 20 watts. He quickly  outgrew this arrangement, however, and moved operations to his factory. The U.S. Department of Commerce granted WLW license #312 on March 2, 1922. In 1923 Crosley established the Crosley Radio Corporation. Thus WLW was born.

At one point, WLW was the most powerful radio station in the world, with an experimental license to broadcast at 500,000 watts. It was truly "the big one," as it is frequently called. President Franklin

Delano Roosevelt flipped a gold-plated telegraph switch in the White House, turning on the power of those 50kW. However, he might just as well have flipped the switch that lifted the floodgates of complaints. Radio stations in Canada and upstate New York immediately complained to the Federal Communications Commission that their signals were being obliterated by WLW's. As a result, WLW was limited to broadcasting at 50,000 watts during the daytime for regular broadcasting. The FCC license card was then amended as follows: "Modification of special experimental authorization to use 500 kw [sic] power from local sunset to 6 A.M. using directional antenna to reduce signal in Niagara to Lockport N.Y. area to equivalent of 50 kw for period ending 8-1-35."

In the 1930s, WLW had an attorney by the name of Ralph Corbett. As a young man, Corbett had been a scholarship student up in his native New York while working his way through law school in an advertising agency during the day and taking classes at night. Corbett vowed to help struggling students whenever he could.

Fresh out of law school, he got a job working as a secretary to the lawyer who helped attorney Clarence Darrow in the Scopes evolution trial. To earn some extra money, he began writing radio scripts on the side and started his own radio marketing and production agency. Powel Crosley started suggesting programming ideas to him; one of those was *Notes on Business*, intended as a morale booster during the Depression. It was a match made in heaven. Another match made in heaven was Ralph and Patricia Ann (Barry) Corbett. It is an understatement to say they made beautiful music together. Pat Corbett had received bachelor's and master's degrees in music from Columbia University. She and Ralph married in 1930 and moved from New York to Cincinnati in 1932 when recruited by WLW.

After a broadcast of *Notes on Business*, a man approached Corbett and proposed an idea to him about a new kind of door chime to replace the ubiquitous buzzer. Corbett lent him $5,000 but the would-be inventor failed. To protect his investment, Corbett took over the plans and named the doorbell NuTone. He fine-tuned the doorbells, trimmed the costs, and made himself a millionaire. He stopped being WLW's attorney in 1937.

Radio was just one facet of Powel Crosley Jr.'s brilliance. He would soon tire of his radio empire and move on to other pastimes. In fact, in 1934 he became majority owner of the Cincinnati Reds baseball team. He would own the Reds until his death in 1961. Even as majority owner, however, he didn't broadcast the games on WLW. The baseball owners strongly felt that broadcasting the games would hurt ticket sales. Crosley also didn't want to waste the airtime on WLW, so he carried the games on WSAI, his smaller station.

In 1934, Crosley bought the Reds to keep them out of bankruptcy and to keep them in Cincinnati. At that point no Major League Baseball team had moved since 1903, but that was no guarantee that it couldn't happen with the right offer. "I have no desire to make money out of the Reds," Crosley said, "and I'm willing to spend money whenever it will keep the club."

That Powel Crosley Jr. was a visionary is no surprise to Cincinnatians who know their history. However, thinking of Crosley as the creator of the worldwide social media movement might be a shocker. And he was only one letter off: WLW.

Before WLW, people's access to the entertainment and news of the day were locally limited and was generally supplied through newspapers and shortwave radio. With WLW's ascendancy into a position in so many living rooms and kitchens in America, suddenly thousands of Americans were sharing experiences at the same time.

WLW launched the careers of many radio, movie, and television stars—some whose names are still familiar today. From the nearby town of Maysville, Kentucky, just east on the Ohio a bit, came two sisters with fabulous voices. Luckily for them, they had faces for more than just radio, because Rosemary and Betty Clooney went on to become featured stars of stage and screen. Rosemary was only 13 when she sang on WLW for the first time. She joined the ranks of

The Clooneys have been a long-time local favorite, often appearing with the Cincinnati Pops under the baton of Erich Kunzel. Depending on your generation, your favorite might be Rosemary, Nick, or George. Here's George for the youngsters among us.

Credit: Cincinnati Symphony and Pops Orchestras

stars including Andy Williams, Jane Froman, Doris Day, and others who got their start at "the Big One." Rosemary and Betty's parents divorced when Rosemary was just 15. Their father stayed here with them, while their mother took their brother Nick and moved to California. Nick Clooney is no stranger to Cincinnatians, as he was a local anchorman for a long time as an adult. However, he is better known nationally as the father of George Clooney—award-winning actor, director, screenwriter, and producer.

WLW should be thought of as "the Big One" for yet another reason, one that some never knew and many will have forgotten: it helped provide the Voice of America to hundreds of thousands of Americans and others throughout the world during World War II. In 1944, President Franklin D. Roosevelt felt that the airwaves were filled with too much anti-American noise. These were the years of Tokyo Rose and Axis Sally and others who were trying to distort the news and disrupt morale of the American forces.

Roosevelt decided to fight fire with fire. He contacted Powel Crosley Jr., who threw his American ingenuity and Cincinnati engineers at the task. They chose a 640-acre site in Butler County, in what is now known as West Chester, and built the Voice of America's Bethany Relay Station. At that site, near WLW's own tower, Crosley's team designed an incredible array and built six 200-kilowatt transmitters. From here, over the next 50 years, Voice of America messages were broadcast to millions of people in 52 languages. However, with the advent of satellite technology, the Voice of America towers became obsolete and were decommissioned in 1995. Bethany Station remains today under the ownership of West Chester Township and is in middle of a $12 million campaign to convert the beautiful Art Deco building into a museum that will preserve the rich history of the Voice of America, wireless radio, and Cincinnati broadcast history.

After creating the magnificent Voice of America installation, Crosley sold it in 1945, along with the Crosley Corporation itself. Crosley began to get the itch to move out of radio and on to other enterprises. He then focused on his other inventions. In the late 1930s, he had already begun experimenting with building a small, gas-efficient car. He introduced the Crosley in 1939, after many failed attempts. He offered a two-cylinder and a four-cylinder version built in Richmond, Indiana. The Crosley cost $325 and got about 50 miles per gallon. It was even sold in department stores.

World War II then got in the way of making the Crosley, just as the war took precedence over other forms of manufacturing. However, after the war, production of the Crosley started up again with a slightly revamped model that reflected some European influences. The new model sold for $850 and got between 30 and 50 miles per gallon. By the end of his run, Crosley was losing $200 on every model sold. Finally he ceased production altogether.

After World War II, Americans were not interested in saving gas and looking like sleek Europeans. They wanted big, ostentatious cars that ate all the unrationed gas their engines desired. In 1946, Powel

Patricia Corbett and her late husband, Ralph, were generous sponsors of the Cincinnati Pops, among many other musical organizations. Here she is seen with Erich Kunzel, right, and trumpeter Doc Severinsen.

Credit: Cincinnati Symphony and Pops Orchestras

Crosley Jr. sold the Crosley Corporation and WLW to AVCO (the Aviation Corporation) for $12 million. When Crosley died in 1961, his name remained only on Crosley Field, the home of the Reds until Riverfront Stadium was completed in 1970. Its, successor, Great American Ball Park, now has a Crosley Terrace in his memory.

Similar to what happened with Powel Crosley's company during World War II, another company that had been affected by the war was Ralph Corbett's NuTone doorbell factory, which converted to anti-aircraft fuse production during the war. At the same time, Corbett lost about a quarter of his workers to military service. During their deployment though, Ralph Corbett wrote 50 letters every week to his workers overseas, hoping that they would want to return to their jobs after their tours were up. Most of them did.

Soon NuTone doorbells were ringing across the country in 50 million homes. Corbett sold the company in 1967 for $30 million and set up trust funds for Pat and their two children. After his family was taken care of, he looked for ways to take care of his community.

Without Ralph and Pat Corbett's having adopted Cincinnati as their home, Cincinnati would be a much quieter place. They helped build, renovate, staff, and fill music halls, auditoriums, and performance venues throughout the tristate: the College-Conservatory of Music's Corbett Auditorium, Riverbend, Music Hall, Northern Kentucky University—all are better for their being here. Ralph did not forget his vow to help other students, either. The Corbetts funded scholarships for students at the School for Creative and Performing Arts, the College Conservatory of Music at the University of Cincinnati, and the Cincinnati Opera.

James Tocco and Patricia Corbett perform at CCM.

Credit: University of Cincinnati Photo Services

Patricia Corbett was a lyric soprano and had performed on radio, on television, and on many stages. The Corbetts' sponsorship of operas was not relegated to just the region, but definitely favored Cincinnati. When Music Hall—Cincinnati's premier musical venue, created for the May Festival—was in need of repair, the Corbetts stepped up with a $6 million gift. The Corbetts' constant support made Cincinnati a major musical venue in the Midwest for performance as well as for musicians learning the ropes. Ralph Corbett died in 1988 at the age of 91; Patricia died in 2008 at the age of 99.

Louis and Louise Nippert were fourth-generation Cincinnatians: he, the great-grandson of P&G co-founder James Gamble; she, born Mary Louise Dieterle, known as Liesel to her friends. Their roots were deep in the complex fabric that makes up Cincinnati. Louis was born in Westwood on Christmas Eve in what was known as the Gamble Mansion on Werk Road. Another Christmas 20 years later would break the family's heart as Louis's brother died from an injury sustained in a University of Cincinnati football game. Still, sports stayed part of their lives, as 50 years later the Cincinnati Reds won back-to-back world championships—with Louis Nippert as the owner.

Before that, though, Louis had already followed in his father's philanthropic footsteps, serving on the board of the Christ Hospital—which

La Bohème performance reception with (left to right) Patricia Corbett, Sue Alexander (Mouch), Louise Nippert, and Paul Bernish (friends of CCM board member and public relations for Kroger). Louis Nippert is seated in front.

Credit: University of Cincinnati Photo Services

his grandfathers had founded in honor of his great-grandmother, Elizabeth Gamble. He served as president of that board for 23 years. He also spent 25 years on the Hamilton County Park Commission. It was he who saved the murals from Union Terminal, then convinced the Cincinnati Historical Society and Museum of Natural History to move to Union Terminal to form the Cincinnati Museum Center.

Mary Louise Dieterle grew up in Clifton, studying music, like her father, George A. Dieterle. She graduated with honors from the University of Cincinnati with a degree in French, but she continued her studies in voice at the College of Music. She even sang a solo with the Cincinnati Symphony once. However, it was not in her nature to seek the spotlight, especially when it came to charitable gifts—and there were many.

After Louis died in November 1992 at the age of 89, Mrs. Nippert continued to be the source of much joy in Cincinnati. She supported

Two recipients of the Lindner family's largesse are the Cincinnati Pops and the Cincinnati Zoo and Botanical Garden. Here, Cincinnati Pops Founder and Director Emeritus Erich Kunzel is seen trying to outrun Sahara, the cheetah. If anyone could do it, he could.

Credit: Cincinnati Symphony and Pops Orchestras

many musical careers through her generous—and often anonymous—gifts to the May Festival, the Matinee Musicale, the Cincinnati Chamber Music Society, the Institute of Fine Arts, the Three Arts Club, and similar organizations.

In 2005, a $30 million gift from the Craig and Frances Lindner and Edyth and Carl H. Lindner Jr. families established the Craig and Frances Lindner Center of HOPE (Helping Other People Excel) in Mason, Ohio, just north of Cincinnati. One of the newest freestanding mental health centers in North America, the Lindner Center of HOPE is operated jointly by the University of Cincinnati Department of Psychiatry, UC Health, and the Lindner Foundation. The Lindner Center of HOPE provides outpatient and inpatient services for adults and adolescents 11 years old and above. It is yet one more way in which the Lindner families have cared for the Cincinnati community.

After years of Carl Lindner's generous support, the University of Cincinnati named its College of Business for Lindner just three months before he died in October 2011 at the age of 92. Carl Lindner's drive and generosity are continued in the hands of his three sons: Carl III, Craig, and Keith.

In 2009 Mrs. Louise Nippert announced that she was making a gift of $85 million to preserve music at the highest possible quality in greater Cincinnati. The Louise Dieterle Nippert Musical

(Continued on page 158)

Fanfares for the Common Folk

The opening notes of Aaron Copland's "Fanfare for the Common Man" are familiar to many. The assertive statements of the timpani, followed by the trumpets, bravely calling out as if to say, "Are you there? I am here!" These notes strike a chord in many Americans.

Cincinnatians might feel a little more resonance than others when they hear those introductory notes, because it was for the Cincinnati Symphony Orchestra that "Fanfare for the Common Man" was written. In 1942, CSO director Eugene Goossens wanted to encourage American composers to write stirring fanfares to raise morale among Americans and American troops. He invited several composers and orchestra leaders to compose small fanfares and to dedicate them to the troops with names such as "Fanfare for the Fallen," "Fanfare for the Heroes," or "Fanfare for Freedom."

It premiered March 12, 1943, during tax season. Both Goossens and Copland thought the timing was excellent to have a piece dedicated to the common man while he (or she) was working hard on taxes. Eighteen premiers were written in response to Goossens' request, but to this day, only Copland's has endured.

What is less commonly known, perhaps, is that this was the second piece that Copland had written for the Cincinnati Symphony Orchestra. Ten days after the December 1941 attack on Pearl Harbor, André Kostelanetz commissioned three composers to write patriotic pieces to honor great Americans for what he hoped would comprise an American gallery. He suggested people such as George Washington, Robert Fulton, and Babe Ruth as worthy of honor.

Kostelanetz chose composers Virgil Thomson, Jerome Kern, and Aaron Copland. Thomson had composed more than 150 such "musical portraits," including one of Aaron Copland, himself. Thomson's method (of the living subjects, which was most of them) was to compose while having the subject of the portrait sit in front of him for inspiration. No one talked during this process—except Fiorello LaGuardia, Thomson's choice for the Kostelanetz commission. (Thomson also chose Dorothy Parker, but his portrait of her was not included in the premiere.)

At first, Copland thought he would honor Walt Whitman for his poetry and his service during the Civil War. However, Jerome Kern chose Mark Twain for his composition, so Copland decided to look beyond a literary figure. He chose Abraham Lincoln and created the incredible "Lincoln Portrait."

The Cincinnati Symphony Orchestra premiered the works in May 1942 with André Kostelanetz conducting and William Adams narrating Copland's piece. Not surprisingly, "Lincoln Portrait" is a favorite of Cincinnatians and has been performed with stellar conductors and narrators. The Cincinnati Pops recorded it in 1987 under the baton of CPO founder and conductor emeritus Erich Kunzel, with Katharine Hepburn narrating. The Pops performed it in 1984 and again in 2009 with narrating honors provided by Neil Armstrong, the first man on the moon. As of this writing, the most recent performance was the 2013 inaugural weekend for music director Louis Langrée, the CSO's tenth director. Legendary poet, author, and dancer Maya Angelou narrated.

Ohioans are not alone in their love of the work, though. It has been performed around the country and even internationally. Multiple Grammys have been awarded to recordings of Copland's "Lincoln Portrait." Copland and the Cincinnati Symphony Orchestra created two works that went from the heartland of the country to the hearts of the people.

(Continued from page 155)

Arts Fund helps to support the Cincinnati Symphony Orchestra, the May Festival, the Cincinnati Opera, the Cincinnati Ballet, and other arts organizations. Despite her advancing years and decreasing mobility, Mrs. Nippert was still a faithful supporter of the organizations, watching every performance from the box at stage right. She was also still a minority owner and loyal supporter of the Cincinnati Reds. When she died in July 2012 at the age of 100, the Symphony and May Festival were in the midst of preparing a special celebration for her.

Both Louis and Louise Nippert received the distinction of being given the Great Living Cincinnatian award, 20 years apart. Their works, their deeds, and their histories represent exactly the type of people who made Cincinnati what it is today.

FINAL WORDS

CINCINNATI CELEBRATED ITS BICENTENNIAL with a year of activities in 1988, ending with a Bicentennial Ball on December 27. Located at Sawyer Point, Bicentennial Commons, part of the Cincinnati Parks, was dedicated in May 1988. The park, designed by Andrew Leicester, encapsulates many symbols of Cincinnati history. A 450-foot earthen bank nestles a replica of the Ohio River from the "Golden Triangle" of the Ohio, Allegheny, and Monongahela rivers at Pittsburgh to where the Ohio River meets with the Mississippi River in Cairo, Illinois. Four flying pig statues atop smokestacks pay tribute to the Porkopolis and its riverboat heritage. Although the Flying Pigs of Bicentennial Commons caused some controversy when they were revealed in 1988, 11 years later, as Cincinnatians were organizing a major marathon for Cincinnati they considered "Queen City Marathon" and "River City Marathon," but finally chose "Flying Pig Marathon" as the best name possible.

Runners agree: not only have they rated the race as having the best name, but also having the best fans and the best giveaways, and being the best race for beginners. *Runner's World* named it one of the top 10 most fun marathons in the country. At the same time, many runners have called it one of the most challenging—but what makes it one of the best is Cincinnatians, themselves. Each year, Cincinnatians line the course, cheering the runners from the first to the last. One-time resident Samuel Clemens (better known as Mark Twain) is often credited with saying that when the end of the world came, he wanted to be back in Cincinnati because we're always 10 (15 or 20) years behind the times. "For better or for worse, what we were is what we are," says Jerome Seiter, a docent at the Cincinnati Museum Center. He could have added "and what we will be." Cincinnati's roots go deep, including strong patterns of immigration, ingenuity, philanthropy, and fierce loyalty to individual and family traditions. Our manufacturing in the *past* was based on iron and steel; our labor was with our hands and the sweat of our backs. Our industry of the *future* will be metal alloys and silicon chips, created in the folds of our brains. Immigration in the past was mostly from Europe: England, Germany, and Ireland; immigration now and in the future will come more from Asia and Latin America. But our new beers will be like our old beers: a return to the small microbrewery where the beer is made in small batches, just as Opa used to make it.

APPENDIX A:

Henry Wadsworth Longfellow's "Catawba Wine"

AFTER TASTING NICHOLAS LONGWORTH'S delicious nectar, Henry Wadsworth Longfellow wrote the following poem in 1854 in its honor:

"Catawba Wine"

This song of mine
Is a Song of the Vine,
To be sung by the glowing embers
Of wayside inns,
When the rain begins
To darken the drear Novembers.

It is not a song
Of the Scuppernong,
From warm Carolinian valleys,
Nor the Isabel
And the Muscadel
That bask in our garden alleys.

Nor the red Mustang,
Whose clusters hang
O'er the waves of the Colorado,
And the fiery flood
Of whose purple blood
Has a dash of Spanish bravado.

For richest and best
Is the wine of the West,
That grows by the Beautiful River;
Whose sweet perfume
Fills all the room
With a benison on the giver.

And as hollow trees
Are the haunts of bees,
For ever going and coming;
So this crystal hive
Is all alive
With a swarming and buzzing and humming.

Very good in its way
Is the Verzenay,
Or the Sillery soft and creamy;
But Catawba wine
Has a taste more divine,
More dulcet, delicious, and dreamy.

There grows no vine
By the haunted Rhine,
By Danube or Guadalquivir,
Nor on island or cape,
That bears such a grape
As grows by the Beautiful River.

Drugged is their juice
For foreign use,
When shipped o'er the reeling Atlantic,
To rack our brains

With the fever pains,
That have driven the Old World frantic.

To the sewers and sinks
With all such drinks,
And after them tumble the mixer;
For a poison malign
Is such Borgia wine,
Or at best but a Devil's Elixir.

While pure as a spring
Is the wine I sing,
And to praise it, one needs but name it;
For Catawba wine
Has need of no sign,
No tavern-bush to proclaim it.

And this Song of the Vine,
This greeting of mine,
The winds and the birds shall deliver
To the Queen of the West,
In her garlands dressed,
On the banks of the Beautiful River.

APPENDIX B:

Presenting Hizzoner, er, Her Honor, the Mayor!

NAME	DATES OF SERVICE
Maj. David Ziegler | **1802–1803 NOTABLE NOTES** Born in what is now referred to as Heidelberg, Germany, Ziegler fought in the Seven Years' War under Frederick the Great, in the Russian army during the Russo-Turkish war, under George Washington at Valley Forge, and was present at the surrender of British General Charles Cornwallis at Yorktown ending the Revolutionary War. Ziegler came to Ohio with Col. Josiah Harmar as a captain in the U.S. Army. He accompanied General St. Clair to the Northwest Territory after receiving his commission as a major. He retired from the army in 1792 and eventually operated a general store in Cincinnati. He was asked to run for a second term as mayor but declined. At this point, the mayor position was referred to as the "president of council." This designation lasted until 1815, at which time a new city charter was voted upon.
Joseph Prince | **1803–1804**
James Findlay (Jacksonian Whig) | **1805–1806**
John S. Gano | **1807**
Martin Baum | **1807 NOTABLE NOTES** Baum's estate is now the Taft Museum of Art. Baum died from influenza and is buried in Spring Grove Cemetery.
Daniel Symmes | **1808–1809 NOTABLE NOTES** Daniel Symmes was the nephew of John Cleves Symmes.
James Findlay | **1810–1811**
Martin Baum | **1812**
William Stanley | **1813**
Samuel W. Davies (Whig) | **1814**
William Corry | **1815–1819**
Isaac G. Burnet | **1819–1831 NOTABLE NOTES** One of a family of brothers, almost all of whom were leaders in the community.
Elisha Hotchkiss | **1831–1833**
Samuel W. Davies | **1833–1843 NOTABLE NOTES** During his 10-year term as mayor, Davies had to deal with the Cincinnati riots of 1836 *and* 1841. He established the mighty waterworks infrastructure, which is both Cincinnati's blessing and burden. Cincinnatians have one of the best waterworks systems in the country, yet because of its age it experiences many problems each winter and spring thaw cycle as very old water mains break under the strain.
Henry E. Spencer | **1843–1851**
Mark P. Taylor (Democrat) | **1851–1853**
David T. Snelbaker (Democrat) | **1853–1855**
James J. Faran (Democrat) | **1855–1857**

NAME	DATES OF SERVICE
Nicholas W. Thomas (Whig)	**1857–1859**
Richard M. Bishop (Democrat)	**1859–1861**
George Hatch (Democrat)	**1861–1863**
Leonard A. Harris	**1863–1866**
Charles F. Wilstach	**1866–1869**
John F. Torrence	**1869–1871**
S. S. Davis (Republican)	**1871–1873**
George W. C. Johnston (Democrat)	**1873–1877**
Robert M. Moore (Republican)	**1877–1879**
Charles Jacob, Jr.	**1879–1881**
William F. Means (Democrat)	**1881–1883**
Thomas J. Stephens (Democrat)	**1883–1885**
Amor Smith, Jr. (Republican)	**1885–1889**
John B. Mosby (Republican)	**1889–1894**
John A. Caldwell (Republican)	**1894–1897**
Gustav Tafel (Democrat)	**1897–1900**
Julius Fleischmann (Republican)	**1900–1905 NOTABLE NOTES** Cincinnati's first Jewish mayor. In this political contest, a Jewish mayor was guaranteed, as his opponent was also Jewish.
Edward J. Dempsey (Democrat)	**1906–1907**
Leopold Markbreit (Republican)	**1908–1909**
John Galvin (Republican)	**1909**
Louis Schwab (Republican)	**1910–1911**
Henry Thomas Hunt (Democrat)	**1912–1913**
Frederick S. Spiegel (Republican)	**1914–1915**
George Puchta (Republican)	**1916–1917**
John Galvin (Republican)	**1918–1921**
George Carrel	**1922–1925**
Murray Seasongood (Charterite)	**1926–1929 NOTABLE NOTES** Murray Seasongood was instrumental in drafting a new city charter reducing the size of city council from 32 to nine members. The city council then elected a mayor from among themselves. This rid the city of the last vestiges of the corrupt George "Boss" Cox regime.
Russell Wilson	1930–1937
James G. Stewart (Republican)	1938–1947
Carl W. Rich (Republican)	**1947 NOTABLE NOTES** Carl Rich was a "cradle to grave" Cincinnatian. He attended Walnut Hills High School and the University of Cincinnati. Besides serving as a Hamilton County prosecutor, on city council, and as mayor, Rich was also the president and chairman of the board of the Cincinnati Royals basketball team.
Albert D. Cash (Charterite)	**1948–1951**

NAME	DATES OF SERVICE
Carl W. Rich (Republican) **| 1951–1953**
Edward N. Waldvogel | 1953–1954
Dorothy N. Dolbey (Charterite) **| 1954 NOTABLE NOTES** Dolbey became Cincinnati's first female mayor when Waldvogel died in office. As vice-mayor, she succeeded him. She did not win the subsequent election, so she returned to council.
Carl W. Rich (Republican) **| 1954**
Charles Phelps Taft, II (Charterite/Republican) | 1955–1957 **NOTABLE NOTES** This C. P. Taft is the nephew of Charles Phelps Taft and the son of William Howard Taft. He served in the army during World War I, returning to college to graduate after the war.
Donald D. Clancy (Republican) **| 1957–1960**
Walton H. Bachrach (Republican) **| 1960–1967**
Eugene P. Ruehlmann (Republican) **| 1967–1971**
Willis D. Gradison Jr. (Republican) **| 1971**
Thomas A. Luken (Democrat) **| 1971–1972**
Theodore M. Berry (Charterite/Democrat) **| 1972–1975 NOTABLE NOTES** Cincinnati's first African American mayor. He had worked in the Office of War Information during World War II. Prior to being elected mayor, he had served as president of the NAACP from 1932 to 1946. He also received many appointments from President Lyndon B. Johnson.
Bobbie L. Sterne (Charterite) **| 1975–1976 NOTABLE NOTES** Sterne was Cincinnati's second female mayor and served a total of 25 years on council. She served as an army nurse during World War II in England, France, and Belgium, attaining the rank of 1st Lieutenant.
James T. Luken (Democrat) **| 1976–1977**
Jerry Springer (Democrat) **| 1977–1978 NOTABLE NOTES** Before Jerry Springer was a nationally known TV host, he was a lawyer, Army reservist, activist for Robert Kennedy, Cincinnati councilman, and newscaster. He gained some notoriety locally when he wrote a check for some 'services' at a brothel. The check bounced.
Bobbie L. Sterne (Charterite) **| 1978–1979**
J. Kenneth Blackwell (Charterite/Republican) **| 1979–1980 NOTABLE NOTES** Ken Blackwell attended Xavier University on a football scholarship, one of the last classes for XU to have a football team. During his term as mayor he had to oversee the city's response to "The Who" disaster at Riverfront Coliseum, where 11 concertgoers lost their lives. He served the state of Ohio as treasurer from 1994 to 1998, when he became Secretary of State. He is also the great-nephew of DeHart Hubbard, the first African American to win an individual gold medal at the Olympics.
David S. Mann (Democrat) **| 1980–1982 NOTABLE NOTES** Mann was returned to council by popular vote in 2013.
Thomas B. Brush (Charterite) **| 1982–1983**
Arnold L. Bortz (Charterite) **| 1983–1984**
Charles J. Luken (Democrat) **| 1984–1991 NOTABLE NOTES** Charlie Luken is the son of former mayor Tom Luken, the first father and son mayor team in Cincinnati.
David S. Mann (Democrat) **| 1991**

NAME	DATES OF SERVICE
Dwight Tillery (Democrat)	**1991–1993**
Roxanne Qualls (Democrat)	**1993–1999**
Charles J. Luken (Democrat)	**1999–2005 NOTABLE NOTES** The city council charter was reformed again to elect the mayor directly by popular vote, as a so-called "strong mayor." Charlie Luken was the first mayor elected under this new system.
Mark Mallory (Democrat)	**2006–2013 NOTABLE NOTES** Mallory is from a family with a tradition of public service. His father, the late William L. Mallory Sr., was the Ohio House of Representatives Majority Leader. Mayor Mallory's brother William Jr. is a Municipal Court judge; his brother Dwane is a Municipal Court judge; his brother Dale is the State Representative in the Ohio House District once held by the Mayor; and his brother Joe is the former Vice Mayor of Forest Park, a city 14 miles northwest of Cincinnati.
John Cranley	**2013–**

APPENDIX C: A Select Representation of Samuel Hannaford's Life's Work

NAME	ARCHITECT &/OR FIRMS	DATE	LOCATION
A. B. Burckhardt Residence, Queen City Nursing Home	Samuel Hannaford	1887	Cincinnati, 400 Forest Ave.
Comments Victorian overtones. Listed on the National Register of Historic Places.			
A. M. Detmer House	Samuel Hannaford	1885	Cincinnati, 1520 Chapel St.
Comments Built for A. M. Detmer, a tailor. Late Victorian style. Listed on the National Register of Historic Places.			
Alexander McDonald House, "Dalvey"	Samuel Hannaford	1881	Cincinnati, Clifton
Comments Victorian Gothic style. Demolished in 1961.			
Alms and Doepke Dry Goods Company	Samuel Hannaford	1878	Cincinnati, Over-the-Rhine (OTR), 222 W. Central Pkwy.
Comments Hannaford designed three houses for William Alms, and one house and two apartment buildings for Frederick Alms. The Alms Hotel was converted from one of the Alms apartment buildings. Listed on the National Register of Historic Places.			
Balch House	Samuel Hannaford	1896	Cincinnati, Greendale Ave.
Comments One of Hannaford's last residential houses built. Listed on the National Register of Historic Places. Queen Anne style.			
Brittany Apartment Building	Samuel Hannaford, Thomas J. & Joseph T. Emery	1885	Cincinnati, 100–104 W. 9th St.
Comments Designed by Hannaford and built by the Emerys. Only the Brittany and the Lombardy exist to this day of Hannaford's downtown apartment buildings. Queen Anne style.			
Camp Washington School (18th District School)	Samuel Hannaford	1882	Cincinnati
Comments Italianate style. Hannaford designed the eastern wing, which was the oldest wing. Demolished in 1994.			

NAME	ARCHITECT &/OR FIRMS	DATE	LOCATION
Capt. George Nelson Stone House	Samuel Hannaford, Samuel Hannaford & Sons	1890	Cincinnati, 405 Oak St.

Comments *Romanesque Revival style. Listed on the National Register of Historic Places. Currently an Alcoholics Anonymous center. After Captain Stone's death, his widow went abroad to spend a year with her stepdaughters. She booked her return trip on the RMS Titanic, but survived the trip.*

Carnegie Library	Samuel Hannaford & Sons	1905–1906	Cincinnati, 3738 Eastern Ave.

Comments *It was built when Cincinnati library trustee James Albert Green visited Andrew Carnegie in New York and asked for funding to build some new libraries. Carnegie had written in "The Gospel of Wealth" that if any city would commit themselves to the upkeep, he would donate to them the funds to build a library. Altogether, he was to thank for nine of Cincinnati's area libraries. This one was originally referred to as the East End Library. Closed in 1959 as a library, it is now the Carnegie Center of Columbia-Tusculum.*

Charles A. Miller House, Steinke House	Samuel Hannaford, Samuel Hannaford & Sons	1890	Cincinnati, 1817 Chase Ave.

Comments *Gothic style. Listed on the National Register of Historic Places.*

Charles B. Russell House, Druffel Building	Samuel Hannaford, Samuel Hannaford & Sons	1890	Cincinnati, Clifton, 3416 Brookline Ave.

Comments *Listed on the National Register of Historic Places.*

Christ Episcopal Church	Samuel Hannaford and Edwin Anderson	1868	Glendale, OH, Sharon, Erie, and Forest Avenues

Cincinnati City Hall	Samuel Hannaford	1888–1893	Cincinnati, downtown

Comments *Richardsonian Romanesque style. Listed on the National Register of Historic Places.*

Cincinnati Memorial Hall	Samuel Hannaford & Sons	1908	Cincinnati, OTR, 1225 Elm St.

Comments *Beaux Arts style. Memorial Hall was created to be a gathering place for veterans and hearing patriotic oratory. Most of the historic memorabilia has been removed and is in the care of preservationists. It is now being used mostly as a small performance venue. Registered as a National Historic Landmark.*

Cincinnati Music Hall	Samuel Hannaford & Sons	1878	Cincinnati, OTR, 1243 Elm St. between 13th and 14th Streets

Comments *Designated a National Historic Landmark in January 1975 and on the U.S. Department of the Interior's National Register since 1970. High Victorian Gothic style. It was built for the longest choral tradition in the Western hemisphere, the Cincinnati May Festival. It is also the home of the Cincinnati Symphony Orchestra, the Cincinnati Pops, and the Cincinnati Opera. It is due to undergo a renovation in 2014/2015 as of this writing.*

NAME	ARCHITECT &/OR FIRMS	DATE	LOCATION
Cincinnati Observatory Building	Samuel Hannaford	1873	Cincinnati, Mt. Lookout
Comments *Neo-Classical/Georgian Revival style. Declared a National Historic Landmark in 1997. It is next to the Ormsby MacKnight Mitchel building, which was also built by Hannaford. The Cincinnati Observatory is the oldest observatory in the United States and has been owned by the University of Cincinnati since 1872.*			
Cincinnati Odd Fellows Temple	Samuel Hannaford & Sons	1891	Cincinnati
Comments *Gothic style.*			
Cincinnati *Times-Star* Building	Samuel Hannaford & Sons	1933	Cincinnati, 800 Broadway
Comments *Art Deco façade. Bought by the* Cincinnati Post, *now used by the Hamilton County juvenile court and other county offices.*			
Cincinnati Work House and Hospital	Samuel Hannaford and Edwin Anderson	1869, demol-ished 1990	Cincinnati, Camp Washington
Comments *Gothic Romanesque style. This was the biggest commission of the Hannaford and Anderson partnership. It was listed on the National Register of Historic Places. At the time it was built, it was considered state of the art.*			
Cincinnati, Hamilton & Dayton Railroad Depot	Samuel Hannaford and Edwin Anderson	1864	Cincinnati, Fifth and Baymiller Streets
Comments *Romanesque Revival style.*			
Cincinnatian Hotel **Comments** *(See "Palace Hotel")*		1882	Cincinnati, downtown
College Hill Town Hall	Samuel Hannaford	1886	Cincinnati, College Hill
Comments *Gothic Revival and Renaissance style. Listed on the National Register of Historic Places. Used by Powel Crosley, Jr., for his early radio experiments.*			
Cummins School **Comments** *Italianate style. Used today as the Walnut Hills Center.*	Samuel Hannaford	1871	Cincinnati, Walnut Hills, 2601 Melrose Ave. and Wm. Howard Taft Rd.
Cuvier Press Club Building	Samuel Hannaford and Edwin Anderson	1862–1963	Cincinnati
Daniel Buell Pierson	Samuel Hannaford and Edwin Anderson	1867	Cincinnati, College Hill, Hillcrest Road at Hamilton
Eden Park Pumping Station No. 7	Samuel Hannaford	1889	Cincinnati, Eden Park

NAME	ARCHITECT &/OR FIRMS	DATE	LOCATION
Eden Park Stand Pipe/ Water Tower	Samuel Hannaford	1894	Cincinnati
Edgecliffe, Thomas Emery residence	Samuel Hannaford	1881	Cincinnati, 2220 Victory Parkway
Comments *Victorian style. Listed on the U.S. National Register of Historic Places.*			
Elsinore Tower	Samuel Hannaford	1883	Cincinnati Eden Park
Comments *Said to be inspired by the castle Kronberg from Shakespeare's "Hamlet." Norman Romanesque style. Listed on the National Register of Historic Places.*			
Emery Hotel	Samuel Hannaford and Edwin Procter	1876	Cincinnati, Vine and 5th Streets
Comments *This building represented the first collaboration between Samuel Hannaford and the Emery family.*			
Emery Row Apartments	Samuel Hannaford	1878	Covington, KY, Scott Blvd.
Emery Theatre	Samuel Hannaford & Sons	1912	Cincinnati
Episcopal Church of Our Savior	Samuel Hannaford and Edwin Procter	1877	Cincinnati, Mt. Auburn, 65 E. Hollister St.
Comments *English Gothic style. It was in this church that Harley Procter was listening to the sermon and thinking about his company's new soap when he heard the Rev. Dr. Rhodes read from Ps. 45:8, "All Thy garments smell of myrrh and aloes, and cassia out of the ivory palaces whereby they have made Thee glad." Thus began P&G's best-selling Ivory soap.*			
Episcopal Church of the Resurrection (now St. Luke's)	Samuel Hannaford and Edwin Procter	1877	Cincinnati, Saylor Park/Fernbank, 7348 Kirkwood Lane
Comments *English Gothic style. Listed on the National Register of Historic Places.*			
Fire Engine Co. #16	Samuel Hannaford and Edwin Anderson	1871	Cincinnati, Walnut Hills, 773 McMillan
Comments *Italianate style.*			
Fire Engine Co. #19	Samuel Hannaford and Edwin Anderson	1871	Cincinnati, Corryville, Short Vine (site of former Zino's Restaurant)
Comments *Italianate style. This, plus Engine #16 firehouse, is the oldest of Hannaford's firehouses still standing. There is some doubt as to whether this was a Hannaford and Anderson collaboration or Hannaford alone, as they dissolved their partnership about this time.*			
First United Methodist Church	Samuel Hannaford & Sons	1891	Middletown, OH

NAME	ARCHITECT &/OR FIRMS	DATE	LOCATION
G. H. Burroughs Residence, Cincinnati Federation of Colored Women's Clubs	Samuel Hannaford & Sons	1888	Cincinnati, 1010 Chapel St.
Comments *Listed on the National Register of Historic Places. Romanesque and Queen Anne influences.*			
George Scott Residence, Mousie House	Samuel Hannaford & Sons	1887	Cincinnati, 565 Purcell Ave.
Comments *Victorian overtones. Listed on the National Register of Historic Places.*			
Glendale Town Hall	Samuel Hannaford and Edwin Procter	1875	Cincinnati, Glendale, 80 E. Sharon Rd.
Grand Hotel	Samuel Hannaford and Edwin Anderson	1874	Cincinnati, Central Ave. between 3rd and 4th Streets
Comments *French Second Empire style.*			
Greene County Courthouse	Samuel Hannaford & Sons	1903	Xenia, OH
H. & S. Pogue Co.	Samuel Hannaford	1886	Cincinnati, 4th St.
Comments *Italianate style.*			
H. & S. Pogue Flats	Samuel Hannaford	1885	Cincinnati, Walnut Hills
H. W. Derby Building	Samuel Hannaford	1887	Cincinnati, 300 W. 4th St.
Comments *Italianate style. Listed on the National Register of Historic Places.*			
Hartwell United Methodist Church	Samuel Hannaford and Edwin Procter	1875	Cincinnati, Hartwell, Parkway Circle and Woodbine Ave.
Henry Powell House	Samuel Hannaford	1882	Cincinnati
Hoffner Masonic Lodge	Samuel Hannaford and Edwin Procter	1885	Cincinnati, Northside, 4120 Hamilton Ave.
Holy Name Church (Zimmerman mansion)	Samuel Hannaford and Edwin Anderson	1860	Cincinnati, Mt. Auburn, 2448 Auburn Ave.
Hooper Building	Samuel Hannaford & Sons	1896	Cincinnati
Comments *Listed on the National Register of Historic Places.*			
John Church Company Building	Samuel Hannaford	1885	Cincinnati, 4th and Elm Streets
Comments *Queen Anne style. Listed on the National Register of Historic Places. Renovated in 1989.*			

NAME	ARCHITECT &/OR FIRMS	DATE	LOCATION
John E. Bell Residence	Samuel Hannaford	1881–1882	Cincinnati 306 McMillan St.
Comments *Destroyed*			
John R. Davey mansion, "Oakwood"	Samuel Hannaford and Edwin Anderson	1869	Cincinnati, College Hill
Comments *Italianate style.*			
Krippendorf-Dittman & Co.	Samuel Hannaford & Sons	1888	Cincinnati, 7th and Sycamore Streets
Lombardy Apartment Building	Samuel Hannaford	1881	Cincinnati, 318–326 W. 4th St.
Comments *Commissioned by Thomas Emery Sons. French Second Empire style. William Howard Taft lived here from 1883 to 1886.*			
Marcus Fechheimer Residence	Samuel Hannaford and Edwin Anderson	1862	Cincinnati, 22 Garfield Pl.
Comments *Renaissance Revival style. Listed on the National Register of Historical Places.*			
Mary A. Wolfe House, Elite Rest and Nursing Home	Samuel Hannaford & Sons	1888	Cincinnati, 965 Burton Ave.
Comments *Listed on the National Register of Historic Places. Romanesque style.*			
McMicken College (original building)	Samuel Hannaford and Edwin Anderson	1874	Cincinnati, Clifton Ave.
Comments *This was the first building for Cincinnati College (later to become the University of Cincinnati). When the college outgrew the original building that Hannaford designed, the College of Medicine took it over. It was later taken over by the College of Law. The building was finally demolished in 1935. Cincinnati native and UC engineering alum Joseph B. Strauss, who constructed the Golden Gate Bridge, collected some of the bricks from the McMicken College building and put them in the base of his Golden Gate Bridge, a concrete homage from a great Cincinnati engineer to a great Cincinnati architect.*			
Miami Medical College	Samuel Hannaford and Edwin Anderson	1866	Cincinnati, OTR, 217 W. 12th St.
Comments *Now used as the Drop Inn Center*			
Monroe County Courthouse	Samuel Hannaford	1905	Woodsfield, OH
Mother of Mercy High School	Samuel Hannaford & Sons	1922	Cincinnati, 3036 Werk Rd.
Mt. Washington Mortuary, Mt. Washington Cemetery	Samuel Hannaford and Edwin Procter	1877	Cincinnati, Mt. Washington
Musik Verein Halle	Samuel Hannaford	1885	Cincinnati, 1115 Walnut St.
Comments *Built for the Cincinnati Männerchor. Sold in 1898 to the Knights of Phythias.*			
Nast Trinity Methodist Church (German)	Samuel Hannaford	1880	Cincinnati, OTR, 1310 Race St.
Comments *Romanesque/English Gothic Revival style.*			

NAME	ARCHITECT &/OR FIRMS	DATE	LOCATION
Norman Chapel at Spring Grove Cemetery	Samuel Hannaford	1880	Cincinnati, Spring Grove Cemetery, Winton Place

Comments *Carolingian Romanesque style*

NAME	ARCHITECT &/OR FIRMS	DATE	LOCATION
Ohio National Guard Armory	Samuel Hannaford & Sons	1886	Cincinnati, 1437–1439 Western Ave.

Comments *Listed on the National Register of Historic Places.*

NAME	ARCHITECT &/OR FIRMS	DATE	LOCATION
Ormsby MacKnight Mitchel Building	Samuel Hannaford & Sons	1904	Cincinnati, Mt. Lookout

Comments *Greek Revival style. Ormsby MacKnight Mitchel was the leading force behind the Cincinnati Observatory and behind the founding of the Cincinnati Astronomical Society. He graduated from West Point with Robert E. Lee. He served as a major general during the Civil War, but contracted yellow fever and died in 1862 and never made it back to his beloved observatory. The town of Fort Mitchell was named in his honor, but an extra "l" was added by mistake when it was incorporated.*

NAME	ARCHITECT &/OR FIRMS	DATE	LOCATION
Our Lady of Mercy Academy and Convent	Samuel Hannford	1897	Cincinnati, Freeman Ave.

NAME	ARCHITECT &/OR FIRMS	DATE	LOCATION
Palace Hotel (now the Cincinnatian)	Samuel Hannaford	1882	Cincinnati, 601 Vine St.

Comments *French Second Empire style. Developed by Thomas Emery, Jr., because he felt that other hotels in town charged too much. The Palace was renamed the Cincinnatian in 1951. It was renovated in 1987 as a luxury hotel and is listed on the National Register of Historic Places.*

NAME	ARCHITECT &/OR FIRMS	DATE	LOCATION
Parkview Manor	Samuel Hannaford	1895	Cincinnati, Clifton, Brookline and Wentworth

Comments *One-time home to renowned Cincinnati political boss George Barnsdale Cox, and later the long-time home to the Pi Kappa Alpha Fraternity at the University of Cincinnati. Parkview Manor is currently under renovation in preparation for the upcoming relocation of the Clifton Branch of the Cincinnati Public Library system.*

NAME	ARCHITECT &/OR FIRMS	DATE	LOCATION
Phoenix Building/ Cincinnati Club	Samuel Hannaford	1893	Cincinnati

Comments *The Phoenix was built as the first private Jewish men's club in Cincinnati.*

NAME	ARCHITECT &/OR FIRMS	DATE	LOCATION
Police Station, District #5	Samuel Hannaford & Sons	1896	Cincinnati, 1024 York St.

Comments *Romanesque Revival style. Listed on the National Register of Historic Places. It was built for the District 5 Mounted Police and served as their headquarters until they relocated to Ludlow in 1957.*

NAME	ARCHITECT &/OR FIRMS	DATE	LOCATION
Probasco Fountain	Samuel Hannaford	1886	Cincinnati, Clifton Ave.

Comments *Henry Probasco worked for Tyler Davidson and was also his brother-in-law. When Davidson died, Probasco inherited the company. Probasco was also mayor of Clifton. At one time the fountain had a public drinking cup attached to it. The main trough was for horses, with the lower basin for dogs.*

NAME	ARCHITECT &/OR FIRMS	DATE	LOCATION
Queen City Club	Samuel Hannaford and Edwin Procter	1876	Cincinnati, 7th and Elm Streets
S. C. Mayer Residence, Rhine Main Building	Samuel Hannaford & Sons	1889	Cincinnati, 1614 Main St.
Comments *French Second Empire style. Listed on the National Register of Historic Places.*			
Sacred Heart Chapel/Sacred Heart Academy	Samuel Hannaford & Sons	1887	Cincinnati, Lafayette Ave.
Comments *Gothic style. Originally built as a chapel for the Windings estate of pork baron William Neff, it was bought by the Sisters of the Sacred Heart. The Neff mansion was converted into a convent and Sacred Heart Academy, which was closed in 1970. The city bought the building and used it for SWAT training. In the 1980s the building again changed hands and was renovated into condominiums. It is listed on the National Register of Historic Places.*			
Salem Methodist Episcopal Church and Parsonage (a.k.a. Salem United Methodist Church)	Samuel Hannaford	1882	Newport, KY, 810 York St.
Comments *Listed on the National Register of Historic Places.*			
Salway residence, superintendent of Spring Grove Cemetery	Samuel Hannaford	1886	Cincinnati, Spring Grove Cemetery
Comments *Listed on the National Register of Historic Places, but demolished in 1984.*			
Samuel Hannaford House	Samuel Hannaford and Edwin Anderson	1865	Cincinnati, Winton Place, 768 Derby Ave.
Comments *Victorian style. Hannaford also designed homes on Derby Ave. for his sons Charles and Harvey. The original Samuel Hannaford house stayed in the Hannaford family until it was sold in the 1940s and subdivided into apartments. It has since been consolidated back into a single-family home.*			
Saxony Apartments Building	Samuel Hannaford, Samuel Hannaford & Sons	1891	Cincinnati, 105–111 W. 9th St. downtown
Schiel School (23rd District School)	Remodeled by Samuel Hannaford & Sons	1911	Cincinnati, 2821 Vine St. ("Short" Vine)
Comments *Remodeled by Hannaford & Sons. Demolished in 2011 after Schiel was combined in 2010 with the School for the Creative and Performing Arts. The land was subsequently used for a mixed-use development.*			
Shubert Theater	Samuel Hannaford & Sons	1892	Cincinnati
Comments *Originally built for the Young Men's Christian Association (YMCA). The block was demolished in 1976.*			

NAME	ARCHITECT &/OR FIRMS	DATE	LOCATION
Sorg Mansion (Later addition done by another architect)	Samuel Hannaford	1886– 1887	Middletown, OH
Comments *Romanesque style. It has since been converted to low-income apartments.*			
Sorg Opera House	Samuel Hannaford	1891	Middletown, OH
Comments *The interior approaches a scaled-down version of Cincinnati's Music Hall, with approximately one-third of Music Hall's capacity.*			
St. George Parish and Newman Center	Samuel Hannaford	1872	Cincinnati, University Heights, 42 Calhoun St.
Comments *German Romanesque style. Listed on the National Register of Historic Places. It has changed hands several times. A fire in January 2008 took down both steeples, which have not been replaced as of this writing.*			
St. Stephen's Episcopal Church	Samuel Hannaford	1887	Cincinnati, Winton Place
Thomas Morrison House	Samuel Hannaford	1875	Cincinnati, 750 Old Ludlow Ave.
Comments *Victorian. Listed on the National Register of Historic Places.*			
Turner Hall	Samuel Hannaford	1884	Cincinnati, Corryville, 2728 Vine St.
Comments *Hannaford remodeled the hall for the Turnverein, the oldest and largest German American Society in Cincinnati. With the anti-German sentiment of WWI, the Turners changed the name of the hall to the North Cincinnati Gymnasium.*			
Van Wormer Library at the University of Cincinnati	Samuel Hannaford	1899– 1901	Cincinnati, University Heights
Vernon Manor	Samuel Hannaford & Sons	1924	Cincinnati
Vigo County Courthouse	Samuel Hannaford	1888	Terre Haute, IN
Walnut Hills United Presbyterian Church	Samuel Hannaford	1885	Cincinnati, Walnut Hills at the inter- section of William Howard Taft and Gilbert Avenues
Comments *This church housed the first integrated worship community in Cincinnati. Both Rev. Dr. Lyman Beecher and Rev. Dr. Calvin Stowe, father and husband, respectively, of Harriet Beecher Stowe, preached from its pulpit. The church was listed on the National Register of Historic Places. After a yearlong fight to save the structure, it was demolished in 2003. All that remains of the church now is the corner bell tower.*			
Walter Field House	Samuel Hannaford	1884	Cincinnati, 3723 Reading Rd.
Comments *Victorian style. Listed on the National Register of Historic Places.*			

NAME	ARCHITECT &/OR FIRMS	DATE	LOCATION
Washington County Courthouse	Samuel Hannaford	1902	Marietta, OH
West Virginia State Capital	Samuel Hannaford and Edwin Anderson	1870	Charleston, WV
Westwood United Methodist Church	Samuel Hannaford	1897	Cincinnati, Westwood
William Miller Department Store	Samuel Hannaford & Sons	1889	Cincinnati, downtown, Race St.
Comments *Now converted to loft apartments.*			
Winton Place Methodist Episcopal Church	Samuel Hannaford, Samuel Hannaford & Sons	1885, parson-age in 1888, Sunday School in 1925	Cincinnati, Winton Place, 700 East Epworth Ave.
Comments *Romanesque style with a Richardsonian arch. This was the Hannaford family's church. Samuel Hannaford met his second and third wives here. His son Charles designed the Sunday School, but construction was delayed because of WWI.*			

BIBLIOGRAPHY

Aaron, Daniel. *Cincinnati, Queen City of the West, 1819-1838.* (Urban Life and Urban Landscape Series) Columbus, Ohio: Ohio State University Press, 1992.

Brown, Dale Patrick. *Literary Cincinnati: The Missing Chapter.* Athens, Ohio: Ohio University Press: 2011.

Englehardt, George Washington. *Cincinnati: A Guide to the Queen City.* Cincinnati: G. W. Englehardt Company, 1901.

Ford, Henry A. and Kate B. Ford. *History of Cincinnati, Ohio, with Illustrations and Biographical Sketches.* Cleveland: L. A. Williams & Co., 1881.

Grace, Kevin. *Legendary Locals of Cincinnati.* Charleston, SC: Legendary Locals, an imprint of Arcadia Publishing, 2011.

Harlow, Alvin F. *The Serene Cincinnatians (Society in America Series).* New York: E. P. Dutton and Company, Inc., 1950.

Herbert, Jeffrey G. *Old Saint Mary's Church, Cincinnati, Ohio: A History of the First 160 Years of Catholic Faith.* Milford, Ohio: Little Miami Publishing Co., 2006.

Horstman, Barry M. *100 Who Made a Difference: Greater Cincinnatians who made a mark on the 20th Century.* Cincinnati: The Cincinnati Post, 1999.

Literary Club, The. *The Literary Club of Cincinnati 1849–1949: Centennial Book.* Cincinnati: The Literary Club, 1949.

Literary Club, The. *The Literary Club of Cincinnati 1849–1974: One Hundred-and-Twenty-fifth Anniversary Volume.* Cincinnati: The Literary Club, 1974.

Literary Club, The. *The Literary Club of Cincinnati 1849–1999: One Hundred-and-Fiftieth Anniversary Volume.* Cincinnati: The Literary Club, 1999.

Marsh, Serge (photographs); text by John Fleischman. *Mid-Century City: Cincinnati at the Apex.* Wilmington, Ohio: Orange Frazer Press, 2007.

McQueen, Keven. *The Axman Came from Hell and Other Southern True Crime Stories.* Gretna, LA: Pelican Publishing Company Inc., 2011.

Milligan, Fred. *Ohio's Founding Fathers*, iUniverse, 2003.

Moore, Gina Ruffin. *Cincinnnati (Black America Series).* Chicago: Arcadia Publishing, 2007.

Morgan, Michael D. *Over-the-Rhine: When Beer Was King.* Charleston, SC: The History Press, 2010.

Nuxhall, Phil. *Beauty in the Grove: Spring Grove Cemetery & Arboretum.* Wilmington, Ohio: Orange Frazer Press, 2009.

Perry, Dick. *Vas You Ever in Zinzinnati?* New York: Doubleday & Co., 1966.

Rolfes, Steven J. *Cincinnati Landmarks (Postcard History Series).* Charleston, SC: Arcadia Publishing, 2012.

Silberstein, Iola Hessler. *Cincinnati Then and Now.* Cincinnati: The League of Women Voters, 1982.

Smiddy, Betty Ann, with the photography of Frank Wilmes. *Cincinnati's Golden Age (Images of America Series).* Charleston, SC: Arcadia Publishing, 2005.

Smiddy, Betty Ann, with support of the Public Library of Cincinnati and Hamilton County. *Cincinnati's Great Disasters (Postcard History Series).* Chicago: Arcadia Publishing, 2007.

Taylor, Robert M. *The Northwest Ordinance, 1787: A Bicentennial Handbook.* Indianapolis: Indiana Historical Society, 1987.

Tolzmann, Don. *Over-the-Rhine Tour Guide: Cincinnati's Historic German District, Over-the-Rhine, and Environs.* Milford, Ohio: Little Miami Publishing Co., 2011.

Writers Program of the Work Projects Administration in the State of Ohio. *Cincinnati: A Guide to the Queen City and Its Neighbors.* Cincinnati: Wiesen-Hart Press, 1943.

Other good resources, if you're interested in the region:

Fanfare, the magazine of the Cincinnati Symphony and Pops Orchestras

The Cincinnati Enquirer

Cincinnati Magazine

UC Magazine

READERS' RESPONSE

Do you think we obviously overlooked someone? Was your family one of the founders of the Queen City? Who do you think played a key role in making Cincinnati what it is today (or what it will be tomorrow)?

Tell us about it! Send an email to the author, care of the publisher, at contact@keencommunication.com and tell us the following:

Whom did we miss?

What did he or she do?

To what significant person was he or she related?

Where can we find documentation of this?

If you include your name and address, you're the only one to tell us this information, and your anecdote is used in a follow-up edition, you'll get acknowledgment in the book and one free autographed copy of that volume.

INDEX

About the Author

WENDY HART BECKMAN is an award-winning free-lance writer and editor. *Founders and Famous Families: Cincinnati* is her seventh work of nonfiction. She has also published more than 300 articles in print and online publications, and has received a baker's dozen of awards for her writing, editing, and desktop publishing.

Wendy's bachelor's degrees are in geology and natural science/

Credit: Tina L. Neyer

technical communications from Virginia Polytechnic Institute & State University and the University of Cincinnati, respectively. She also has a master's degree in English from UC with a graduate certificate in professional writing.

She has taught English, business writing, and scientific and technical writing at the University of Cincinnati and cultural diversity at Miami University. She frequently offers workshops, from a few hours in length to weekend-long retreats, for writers who wish to get published.

Besides writing, Wendy's passion lies in singing. For 10 years she was a member of the Cincinnati May Festival Chorus, the oldest continuous choral tradition in the Western hemisphere. When she's not engaged in writing or singing, she can be found with one of her paintball teams, working on behalf of the nonprofit that she co-founded, Athletes Joined Against Spondylitis. She lives in Cincinnati with her husband and three sons.